THE YEAR
CANADIANS
LOST * MINDS
THEIR
AND FOUND THEIR COUNTRY

THE CENTENNIAL OF
1967

TOM HAWTHORN

Douglas & McIntyre

DEDICATION

To John and Nellie, who won life's jackpot
by being born in Canada

More than 100 million copies of this 5¢ commemorative stamp were issued. It depicts Canada's land
mass on the globe, the new national flag adopted
two years earlier, and Stuart Ash's centennial
symbol. *Photo: Canada Post*

Douglas and McIntyre (2013) Ltd.
P.O. Box 219, Madeira Park, BC, V0N 2H0
www.douglas-mcintyre.com

Edited by Cheryl Cohen
Indexed by Kyla Shauer
Design by Diane Robertson

Printed and Bound in Canada

Douglas and McIntyre (2013) Ltd. acknowledges the support of the Canada Council
for the Arts, which last year invested $153 million to bring the arts to Canadians
throughout the country. We also gratefully acknowledge financial support from the
Government of Canada through the Canada Book Fund and from the Province of
British Columbia through the BC Arts Council and the Book Publishing Tax Credit.

LIBRARY AND ARCHIVES CANADA CATALOGUING IN PUBLICATION
Hawthorn, Tom, author

   The year Canadians lost their minds and found their country : the Centennial
of 1967 / Tom Hawthorn.

Includes bibliographical references and index.
Issued in print and electronic formats.
ISBN 978-1-77162-150-2 (softcover).--ISBN 978-1-77162-151-9 (HTML)

   1. National characteristics, Canadian. 2. Nationalism--Canada.
3. Canada--Centennial celebrations, etc. I. Title.

FC623.C4H39 2017   971.064'4   C2017-901820-5
                                 C2017-901821-3

Contents

Preface

THE CANADA OF 1968 was a profoundly different place than the Canada of 1966. The year in between, when Canadians took hesitant steps toward celebrating what we had achieved, led to a renewed interest in the question of who we were and where we were going. All that was to come—including Trudeaumania; the state getting out of the bedrooms of the nation; women demanding an equal place in society; and massive changes to the population through immigration—was made possible during Centennial Year. It was the beginning of a new sense of national identity, one in which race, culture and language would play lesser roles than we had become accustomed to in the country's first century.

We invited the world to celebrate with us in 1967. By the time the final birthday candle had been blown out, we had more of a global perspective. The Canada of 2017 owes more to decisions made in the wake of 1967 than to the negotiations conducted in 1867.

The Year Canadians Lost Their Minds and Found Their Country is not a history, nor an exercise in sentimental longing. Many Canadians—the young, which is to say anyone under fifty; and new arrivals, which is to say anyone who immigrated here any time in the past half-century—have no memory

A birthday party for children was held on Parliament Hill on July 1 featuring clowns, balloons, dancers and a Punch-and-Judy puppet show. Each child got a cupcake, too.
Photo: Library and Archives Canada

of what happened in 1967. What lies between these covers are stories that will help us to appreciate the audacity of those who sought the grand gesture in experiencing their country. One does not set off down the Trans-Canada Highway on foot, as young Hank Gallant did, or attempt to canoe and portage a continent, without desiring to test oneself against a majestic, unforgiving land.

This book is not so much a single narrative as a scrapbook of vignettes, anecdotes and factual tidbits (okay, trivia) that are loosely divided into sections after the opening overview essay, "The Giddy Year." I hope that the collection serves as a portrayal of an unforgettable, optimistic time, one to be relived by those in their fifties and older, and one to be explored by those who missed out on the fun.

Before I started this project, I had never heard of British Columbia homesteader Ida DeKelver, who trekked—accompanied by a pair of donkeys—from British Columbia through the Rockies to her Saskatchewan birthplace during Centennial Year.

Sometimes, I came across a coincidence that made Canada seem a small place. Eugene Boyko, the filmmaker responsible for the panoramic aerial view that gained the centennial project *Helicopter Canada* an Oscar nomination, had earlier done a short documentary on a Montreal housing project. As a boy, I had watched from this same housing project the building of a subway that would carry visitors to Expo 67. The International and Universal Exhibition would come to be remembered as a highlight of Canada's Centennial Year.

—

ONE OF MY earliest memories: I am looking out our second-storey apartment window at men and equipment working in the street below. It is the mid-1960s and we live in the Habitations Jeanne-Mance housing project near downtown Montreal. These modernist apartment buildings have recently replaced a red-light district, demolished in the post-war, slum-clearing reform movement. The street below has wooden stockades erected along both sides of the roadway like a long narrow fort.

Below the blacktop, tunnel-digging machinery bores through rock. The Metro is being built. Three blocks away, a huge hole in the ground marks the site of the main terminus of the new system, where two lines are to converge. (And, after Expo 67 is announced, a third line will be added beneath the other two.) The dirt dug from beneath our street will be dumped into the St. Lawrence River to help form the islands that will be home to the world's fair.

The elevated monorail at Expo 67 gave riders a breathtaking tour through Buckminster Fuller's geodesic dome, which was home to the United States pavilion. *Photo: Library and Archives Canada*

A few years later, as Expo 67 opens in April, we are living in the leafy Notre-Dame-de-Grâce neighbourhood in a small apartment building on a cul-de-sac sandwiched between train tracks and an escarpment. The world's fair is impossible to ignore. It is on television and in the newspapers, talked about in class and featured in a wall-sized poster at our nearest coffee shop.

From some vistas downtown, I can see the Buckminster Fuller geodesic glass dome that is the United States pavilion and I can see the Union Jack colours painted atop the tower of Britain's pavilion. It is as though Disneyland and the Beatles are both but a few Metro stops away. I am obsessed in the way only a seven-year-old boy can be obsessed. I can identify pavilions from their

Centennial celebrations and projects can be found in even the smallest hamlet. In Sovereign, Saskatchewan, residents built a fire hall in 1967. The building, now weathered, still sports a wooden centennial symbol. *Photo: Gord McIntyre*

silhouettes and know impossible amounts of trivia about the fair. I beg my parents to take me. They are averse to crowds and despise queuing, so there is resistance. Finally, though, it is agreed we will go.

The great day arrives! It is a weekend, as my father works weekdays packing and shipping lingerie in a factory in the heart of the *shmata* industry. We cross the train tracks through a hole in the fence before catching the bus along Sherbrooke Street to the Alexis Nihon Plaza, where we make a stop to buy bread, cheese and processed meat for a picnic lunch. We have heard that food is expensive at Expo. As well, my father has come up with some contraption in his pocket to ensure that his wallet cannot be eased out by a pickpocket. Then it is onto the Metro, the Green Line from Atwater running below our old apartment to Berri-DeMontigny (now Berri-UQAM), where we transfer to the Yellow Line by riding escalators deep, deep below the surface. One stop later we arrive at Île Sainte-Hélène and pay $7.50 (about $53 in today's money) for day passports for a family of four: admission into a real-life land resembling that of the animated sitcom *The Jetsons.*

THE YEAR CANADIANS LOST THEIR MINDS AND FOUND THEIR COUNTRY

A monorail soars overhead. A hovercraft noisily bumps across the river. A giant Alexander Calder sculpture looms over a square, making steel look as lithe as a dancer. I speak to my mother on a newfangled videophone at the Telephone Pavilion, a marvel from Dick Tracy comics that now is available to everyone with a smart phone anywhere on the planet. We zip on the Expo Express train to tour Habitat.

My other lingering memory is of the Israeli pavilion, where this boy had so many questions about that boy in the photograph with his arms in the air and soldiers with guns. History seemed so much harsher than the utopian future of all races, all creeds living in harmony—or at least expressing animosity only via architectural grandiosity and curatorial chauvinism. (Looking at you, Soviet and American pavilions).

—

IN MONTREAL, AT least, Expo dominated Centennial Year. I'm pretty sure we cut out triangles of coloured construction paper in our Grade 2 class to form Stuart Ash's simple but indelible centennial symbol. Quebec Premier Daniel Johnston's nationalist government was not putting much effort into promoting Canada's hundredth birthday. It was television that brought the national celebrations into our living room, as into the homes of so many others, a portal that allowed all of us to share in the celebration.

1

The Giddy Year

1967 Before, During and After the World's Fair

FOR ONE HAPPY, giddy, insane year, a normally reserved people decided to hold a blockbuster party from coast to coast to coast. The occasion: Canada's one hundredth birthday. The event to be celebrated was spectacularly unexciting; the nation was founded not through blood and revolution, but through discussion and negotiation by bewhiskered men in nineteenth-century frock coats sitting around tables for palaver. In 1967, which popular historian Pierre Berton called "the last good year," Canadians compensated for the ordinariness of their beginnings by holding a year-long, blowout celebration to which we invited the world. Those who experienced it will never forget the feeling.

At first, Canadians showed little interest. The announcement of a federal program to plan the celebration was met with silence and indifference. The planning was "top down," federal bureaucrats determining appropriate ways to mark the occasion: an unsurprising approach in a nation dedicated to "peace, order and good government." The centrepiece was to be a World's Fair held on man-made islands in the middle of the St. Lawrence River off Montreal, a Category One exposition set to run from April to October with pavilions from nations on every continent. Some predicted that Canada's uncertain

In February, Canada Post released a new definitive series with the Queen featured on five stamps costing from 1¢ to 5¢. The higher denominations (from 8¢ to $1) featured paintings by the Group of Seven and Tom Thomson, whose 1917 work *The Jack Pine* graced the 10¢ stamp. *Photo: Canada Post*

step onto the world stage would be a fiasco, an expensive exercise in hubris and embarrassment sponsored by a population unsure of their purpose and uncomfortable with all the attention. The English-language newspapers insisted on referring to a Montreal World's Fair, even campaigning against the jazzy name "Expo 67," thinking it sounded like a new cigarette.

Centennial Commissioner John Fisher, nicknamed "Mr. Canada" because of his time on CBC Radio, urged Canadians to mark the centenary as best they could. "The Centennial belongs to you," he announced. "It does not belong to governments. Do something. It doesn't matter how small your effort is."

A funny thing happened in the weeks leading to New Year's Day 1967. Canadians embraced the official plans for a celebration and, encouraged by government largesse, began making plans of their own. Reminders of centennial projects can be found in nearly every town and hamlet in the land, from centennial Stadium in Victoria, British Columbia, to the Centennial

Firehall in Sovereign, Saskatchewan, to the Arts and Culture Centre in St. John's, Newfoundland and Labrador. There are Centennial Secondary Schools, Centennial Halls and Centennial Parks scattered across the land.

More impressively, individual Canadians decided on their own—and on their own dollar—to mark the occasion in unique ways. An Edmonton bush pilot flew to an isolated ice floe to plant the centennial flag at the North Pole. Another Edmonton man, a house painter by profession, nearly died trying to drive a dog sled from Tuktoyaktuk to Alberta's capital. Climbers conquered the virgin mountains of the Centennial Range in the Yukon. A brigade of vintage cars, led by a Model T, crawled across the land from Victoria to Expo 67. Hank Gallant, a fisherman from Prince Edward Island, decided to walk from Victoria to St. John's; when he got to the nation's capital, he was arrested for vagrancy. In Nanaimo, a flamboyant mayor dressed as a pirate to inaugurate a bathtub race across Georgia Strait to Vancouver. (The winner claimed a one-hundred-dollar cash prize. Happily, no one drowned.) In Toronto, the expatriate community from the West Indies held the first celebration of Caribana.

Teams representing every province and both territories competed in an arduous, 5,283-kilometre trek by canoe and portage along the voyageur route from the headwaters of the North Saskatchewan River to Montreal. Fourteen Mi'kmaq from Nova Scotia completed a forty-five-day canoe trip to commemorate a peace treaty between their people and the Iroquois of Quebec. Jesuits made a pilgrimage retracing the missionary route connecting Montreal to Midland, Ontario.

A Centennial Train crossed the land, a rolling museum featuring six display cars. Truck-driven Centennial Caravans travelled the winding highways to isolated communities. A barge brought the centennial message to northern people along the Mackenzie River.

The Centennial touched every aspect of Canadian life. There were centennial coins, centennial postage stamps, centennial licence plates, a new centennial typeface, a centennial logo and a Centennial Hymn.

In Winnipeg, the greatest athletes in the hemisphere gathered for the Pan American Games. New public buildings were constructed in Ottawa and in every provincial capital. In St. Paul, Alberta, citizens built a landing pad for UFOs, a tongue-in-cheek tourist attraction that has kept the prairie crossroads on the map for a half-century.

Centennial Year even had a soundtrack. On the very first day of the new year, Gordon Lightfoot introduced his epic "Canadian Railway Trilogy" to a national CBC Television audience. A film at the Ontario pavilion at Expo 67 introduced

The Confederation Train is here

The Confederation Caravan is here

The Confederation Train, a rolling museum on wheels, stopped at sixty-three cities across Canada. Smaller cities, towns and hamlets were visited by one of the Confederation Caravans, which had similar exhibitions to the train. *Photo: Library and Archives Canada*

the catchy tune "A Place to Stand (Ontar-i-ar-i-ar-i-o)." An anthem by tunesmith and band leader Bobby Gimby, recorded by a children's chorus known as the Young Canada Singers, drowned out the song that had won the $5,000 contest for an Expo 67 theme song ("Hey Friend, Say Friend"). Gimby's "Canada," better remembered as "Ca-na-da," sold an astonishing number of 45-rpm records and a remarkable amount of sheet music. Dozens of other tunes were recorded and released to mark the centenary and the world's fair. Yet, at the end of the year, Bobby Gimby's novelty song was the only Canadian record among the Top 100 in sales and airplay.

It is hard to capture, a half-century later, how little Canada had mattered to the world and how little we'd regarded our own efforts at self-expression. Canada was said to have no literature, no cuisine, little culture and nothing worthwhile to say in popular movies, music or theatre. We were hewers of wood and drawers of water who were taught old folk songs about fishing and lumberjacking, which truly seemed foreign if you were growing up in an apartment in the city. We were ignored on the world stage, our important contribution to the defeat of Nazism overlooked by British and American films and books. What was Canadian? Nothing of importance. It could seem as though the most recent Canadian contribution to popular culture had been the birth of the Dionne quintuplets decades earlier.

Now, Canadian music in all genres provides a soundtrack for the globe. Canadian actors win acclaim and even Canadians are unaware which young acting or musical star is Canadian. A Canadian has won the Nobel Prize for Literature (and, no, it is not Saul Bellow, born in Montreal but regarded as a product of Chicago). In Centennial Year, we discovered that we had a talent for humour, for storytelling, for design, for athletics, for innovation.

"It has changed the country," said John Fisher, who had begun preaching the cause of a centennial celebration back in 1949. "There's a new emphasis on Canadianism now, and it was the response of the little people that brought it about."

Those heady days set the pattern for the Canada to come. Without the transcontinental expeditions of 1967, would Terry Fox have been inspired to launch his own unlikely run for cancer research just thirteen years later? Without the stirrings of 1967, would the "I Am Canadian" beer advertising campaign even have been conceivable? The unabashed nationalism on display during the 2010 Olympics was a successor to the national pride on display in 1967. It is hard, too, to imagine that Canada would become an accepting place for immigrants and refugees from around the globe without our first having played host to the world at Expo 67. How much of our own global

A scarf celebrating Montreal and Expo 67 and a mug with the centennial symbol were among the thousands of souvenirs available in 1967. Many can still be found in attics, basements, thrift shops and garage sales. *Photo: Colleen Proctor*

trekking—maple leaves proudly sewn on backpacks—has been inspired by getting passports stamped at national pavilions located on two islands in the middle of a river?

"We thought something magical might happen if Canadians were brought together in a common enterprise," said Peter Ackroyd, who directed the Centennial Commission's publicity and advertising service. He was right. It helped us realize we had something to say and something to share.

Centennial Year was also a moment when the ancestors of colonial settlers and immigrants alike were challenged to confront the legacy of Canada's relationships with First Nations, Métis and the Inuit. The opera *Louis Riel* renewed interest in the Métis leader. Displays at the Indians of Canada pavilion at Expo 67 demanded that the rest of the country confront a shared history. Chief Dan George's searing soliloquy, "Lament for Confederation," delivered before a full house at Vancouver's Empire Stadium on Dominion Day in 1967, heralded a new militancy.

—

Children enjoy a train ride at La Ronde, the amusement park that opened with Expo 67. Unlike the pavilions, the park was designed to be a permanent attraction. *Photo: Library and Archives Canada*

THE GREATEST ACHIEVEMENT of the year of celebrations was a seductive awakening of spirit, as the author Pierre Berton noted. Judy LaMarsh, the hard-charging politician who oversaw centennial planning as secretary of state, was a ubiquitous figure in 1967, appearing in formal wear at grand state events and in boots, in the muck, at small-town ribbon cuttings. A frequent target of derision at the time and somewhat forgotten today, LaMarsh deserves credit as a trailblazer who endured daily sexist humiliations and simply ploughed on. "We cast off the bonds of our conformity, and slipped out of our cloak of grey anonymity forever," she wrote in her memoir. "The year 1967 changed us all profoundly, and we will never look back."

2 Official Centennial

From Fire, Bells and Coins to Go-Go Tartan

T HE LIGHTING OF the Centennial Flame in the final hours of 1966 and the pealing of bells around the world in the opening minutes of 1967 were early indicators that Centennial Year was an officially sanctioned time for celebration. The message was clear: it would be a year of spectacle and wonderment. The world's fair was set to open in four months; a Confederation Train was on schedule to travel from the capital city to Victoria, British Columbia, and then turn around for a slow, transcontinental return; a caravan of eight trucks would criss-cross the country as a mobile museum; and all kinds of cultural, sports and military events would unfold.

Ready, Set, Go!

CENTENNIAL FLAME

It was just past seven o'clock on New Year's Eve on Parliament Hill. Organizers chose not to wait until midnight to perform the ceremony, so as to permit children to watch on television and to attend in person. A large crowd, bundled against the winter chill and stomping booted feet on snow to stay warm, watched on a large, wide-angle screen as the monarch delivered her annual message.

Prime Minister Lester Pearson used a long pole to ignite the natural gas–fuelled burner of the Centennial Flame on December 31, 1966, a ritual watched by a national television audience. The pole itself was lit out of sight by an ordinary match. *Photo: Library and Archives Canada*

"In 1967 the world will be looking at Canada as it never has done before," the Queen said. "Perhaps you do not always realize yourselves how much your own achievements have made you worthy of this attention from other nations. As your Queen, I trust that all Canadians, in every region and province, will also use this centennial year to reflect upon the nation's history and to consider how unique and splendid it has been."

At homes across the nation, the viewing audience could hear the Queen clearly. In Ottawa, her image was sharp on the screen, though her voice was dulled away from the podium. Most of those in attendance would learn what she had to say only by reading her statement in the newspaper after the holidays.

"Canada's example," she continued, "gives hope to free men everywhere that this world of such vast cultural and political and social diversity can also learn to live in harmony and peace."

A prayer followed, and then the singing of the official Centennial Hymn.

It was time to light the Centennial Flame, which was to burn throughout the year of celebration. The flame was fed by a natural gas jet spurting from a fountain built in the forecourt of Parliament Hill, with the majestic Peace

The Centennial Flame on Parliament Hill was built from red Canadian granite. Bronze armorial bearings for the ten provinces and two territories that made up Confederation in 1967 were installed within the basin. *Photo: Michel Rathwell / Flickr*

Tower looming behind. Organizers had considered how best to spark the fire, debating the merits of using National Research Council laboratories, or striking steel against flint. In the end, they settled upon an ordinary matchstick. After all, the famous E.B. Eddy match factory had been established on the other side of the Ottawa River more than a decade before Confederation. Out of sight of the television cameras, an ordinary match lit the flammable end of a long pole. Prime Minister Lester Pearson, a hat on his head and gloves on his hands, was joined at the fountain by his fur-coat-clad secretary of state, Judy LaMarsh, a free-spirited maverick who would travel to every corner of the country during the year.

The monument housing the Centennial Flame was built of red Canadian granite. Bronze coat of arms for the ten provinces and two territories that made up Confederation in 1967 were installed within the basin. (A third territory, Nunavut, has since been carved out of the Northwest Territories.) The date on which each joined Canada has been engraved on the lip of fountain. The monument is surrounded by paving stones of Tadoussac gneiss from Quebec.

Pearson leaned over the fountain to ignite the Centennial Flame. "O Canada" was sung and the prime minister read some remarks. Then torches were lit from the flame, to be carried to fifteen municipalities in the Ottawa region.

INTERNATIONAL BELLS—AND DOORBELLS

A bell rang in Japan at midnight local time and an hour later a bell rang in the Philippines at the famous Wack-Wack Golf and Country Club in Manila. An hour after that, a bell rang on the island of Sumatra in Indonesia.

In Israel, Reverend Gonzague Hudon, a Franciscan monk from Quebec, chimed the bells at St. Joseph's Church in Nazareth, the village in which Jesus was raised.

Ships at dock and in the harbour of Helsinki tolled their bells, while the town bells rang through the midnight air in Brouage, birthplace of Samuel de Champlain, the tintinnabulation echoing from Finland to France.

BONFIRE OF THE LAVATORIES

Flame was also the theme for the launching of centennial celebrations in tiny Bowsman, Manitoba.

The village, about five hundred kilometres northwest of Winnipeg, had recently installed a sewage treatment plant. With houses at last hooked up to running water, Bowsman's 504 residents no longer had need of the privies where they had attended to nature's business over the years. It was suggested that the outcast outhouses be destroyed as a centennial project.

On the final day of 1966, the outbuildings were decorated with balloons and toilet-tissue streamers, loaded onto the backs of trucks and paraded through the village to the filtration plant. Some local notables were playfully honoured as members of the village's "Privy Council." After a rendition of "Auld Lang Syne," Reverend Jim Liles, a United Church minister, read an ode he'd penned, which began: "The time has come to destroy friends who have held up their ends through the years." With that, the thirty-three discarded outhouses were set alight in a bonfire of the lavatories.

There were headlines around the continent. "In Bowsman, the End Justified the Means," said the Winnipeg Tribune. "Funeral Pyre of Privies Leaves Cold Ashes Behind," the Vancouver Sun cheekily reported.

Three years later, on the centennial of Manitoba's joining Confederation, a cairn was built to celebrate what had come to be called the Biffy Burn. Made of field stones with a brass plaque, the cairn was topped by the wooden model of an outhouse.

In the picturesque village of Gomshall, England, a mill town on the Tillingbourne River, Alfred Dowling did not have access to a church bell, so the eighty-seven-year-old instead rang the doorbells of his neighbours. When informed of the plan, Paul Drolet of St. Paul, Alberta, had approved. "The neighbours may not appreciate it until they find out why it is being done," he said, "but it is a tremendous idea."

Drolet led a campaign from the Alberta town to encourage people around the world to chime bells to greet Canada's centennial at midnight on January 1, 1967. The Centennial Commission called for bells to be rung for five minutes at midnight on New Year's and on July 1. Since most bells are in the control of municipal, religious or seafaring authorities, the commission could but make a suggestion, so the townspeople in St. Paul made it one of their centennial projects to spread the word.

They arranged for ships in the Atlantic to sound their bells before churches began pealing the arrival of the New Year in St. John's, Newfoundland. Five and a half hours later, bells rang on the opposite coast, in Victoria, British Columbia. Meanwhile, the cacophonous celebration was marked in such places as Centennial, Nova Scotia, and Milestone, Saskatchewan—not to mention Carillon, Quebec.

In Winnipeg, the four new bells in the twenty-nine-metre tower of St. Paul's College sounded for the first time. Down the Trans-Canada Highway in Brandon, the big bell atop the fire station, cast in 1902 and dedicated to mark the coronation of King Edward VII, rang out across the Wheat City. It was joined by the 111-bell carillon at St. Matthew's Cathedral, the carillon chimes at First United Church (donated by Arma Sifton and later moved to the International Peace Gardens on the border), and the bells at St. Joseph's Polish National Catholic Church and St. Mary's Anglican Church—the latter a Canadian Pacific Railway engine bell installed in honour of the occupation of so many of the parishioners. As well, railway engines in the city sounded their diesel horns, while the siren sounded atop the Brandon Hospital for Mental Diseases.

Our American neighbours took part, too, as the town crier paraded through the streets of Canton, Ohio, while Ed Murphy sounded the Freedom Bell in Fairbanks, Alaska.

CBC CURTAIN-RAISER

At 7:30 p.m. on New Year's Day, those who wanted to get into the centennial spirit early could turn to CBC TV for a ninety-minute variety show called "One Hundred Years Young," a curtain-raiser for the centennial celebrations.

The biggest show of its kind ever attempted to that time by the Canadian Broadcasting Corporation, the program was hosted by Austin Willis, the Halifax-born actor who appeared in the opening scene of the James Bond movie *Goldfinger*.

Broadcast in colour, the fast-paced show included performances by the comedians Don Harron, Sylvia Lennick and the duo Wayne and Shuster. Among the musical acts were Juliette, folk singer Gordon Lightfoot, Quebec singer Robert Demontigny and Vancouver folk rock band 3's a Crowd, who would go on to perform at the Ontario pavilion at Expo 67. The conductor Ivan Romanoff led a forty-person orchestra. Other acts included the tenor Alan Crofoot, who had created Mr. Bumble in the Broadway production of *Oliver!* and the seventy-voice choir of Appian Public School in Toronto.

"A big-budget spectacular," wrote Sandy Gardiner, television critic for the Ottawa Journal, who continued:

> *The emphasis was on a fast-moving brilliantly staged production, full of songs, dancing and all the gaiety of a New Year's party condensed for the tube. The big surprise was that the hour and a half managed to maintain the pace, showing that Canada can equal and, at times, surpass the US in this field.*

For all the praise, Gardiner actually preferred the hour-long quiz show that followed the variety special. Co-hosted by journalists Donald Gordon and June Callwood, "Canadian History Test" challenged viewers' knowledge of Canada's past with appearances by former Governor General Vincent Massey, NDP leader Tommy Douglas, Conservative leader John Diefenbaker and Prime Minister Lester Pearson. Viewers at home could write their answers to twenty questions on blank spaces in advertisements placed in local newspapers.

The high-brow quiz show was followed by a special edition of *Sunday*, hosted by the folksinger Ian Tyson at his ranch near Newtonville, Ontario. (He'd later record a song titled "Newtonville Waltz.")

One long (by television standards) segment would linger in popular memory, though it seemed to receive scant attention in the reviews of the day. The variety show included the debut of a Lightfoot original. Backed by the orchestra and a chorus of dancing, hammer-wielding navvies, the number, "Canadian Railroad Trilogy," lasted nearly nine minutes.

In his book *The History of Canadian Rock 'n' Roll*, music historian Bob Mersereau quoted Lightfoot as recalling that Bob Jarvis of the CBC had asked if he would write a song about the railroad for the New Year's Day special that CBC TV would be broadcasting:

The centennial symbol graces the centre of the Centennial Flame, which was first lit on December 31, 1966. The flame was supposed to be dismantled after a year. A campaign by a radio station led to its preservation. It remains a favourite of visitors to Parliament Hill. *Photo: Eduardo Zárate / Flickr*

I said, "About how long?" "As long as you want to make it.". . . Then he sent me a book to read about William Cornelius Van Horne, who was in charge of building the railway. Three days later, I had the song.

Unexpected Treasure and Caffes

In the first week of 1967, visitors to the Centennial Flame tossed $5.71 in change into the surrounding pool. (That's about $40 in today's money.) After a fortnight, the total was $42.41 and growing, a heavy haul in the days before loonies and toonies. At first, it was unclear what to do with this unexpected windfall. Now, about six thousand dollars a year in coins is fished from the fountain, the money donated for research on disabilities. The monument itself—originally intended to be dismantled after a year—was left in place after a campaign led by a local radio station, and today remains a popular place for tourists to take photographs and to make a wish.

———

LET * THE FESTIVITIES BEGIN: *

NEW YEAR'S EVE PROGRAM FOR PARLIAMENT HILL

6:55 p.m. —   Prime minister and party walk from Centre
                  Block to dais

7 p.m. —   Queen's message

7:05 p.m. —   Centennial Prayer

7:09 p.m. —   Centennial Hymn

7:14 p.m. —   Prime minister lights
                  Centennial Flame

7:15 p.m. —   Massed choirs sing "O Canada"

7:18 p.m. —   Prime minister's message to the country

7:25 p.m. —   Mayors and reeves from fifteen municipal-
                  ities light torches from the flame and pass
                  them to their couriers

7:30 p.m. —   Prime minister exits

7:31 p.m. —   Couriers leave the grounds, carrying the torch
                  by foot, by car, and by horse-drawn carriage
                  to nearby municipalities, to ring the National
                  Capital area with bonfires of friendship

AFTER A FORTNIGHT of centennial celebrations, the Canadian Press catalogued a series of minor disasters for a gaffe-filled national birthday, noting that the first prime minister's name had been misspelled on a banner; the New Year's Eve crowd on Parliament Hill could not hear the Queen's or the prime minister's address; and fifteen hundred revellers who had paid three dollars each to attend the party that night at Ottawa's new Centennial Centre had to stand in line at the one wicket selling bar tickets—making it the toughest place in Canada to get a drink on New Year's Eve.

Editorialists griped about the sound system on Parliament Hill.

Even the flame, fed by natural gas as protection against the harsh Ottawa winter, would come under fire. It sputtered out in February, though it soon was reignited by workmen.

One catastrophe was averted hours before the New Year's Eve broadcast when workmen testing television floodlights and sparks from a generator's exhaust pipe ignited a tarpaulin and planks at the rear of a dump truck. The flames on the lighting truck were extinguished before firefighters arrived.

New Year's Service

CBC Radio broadcast a Centennial Ecumenical Service at 11 a.m. on New Year's Day. It was conducted by a number of dignitaries:

- Maurice Cardinal Roy, Archbishop of Quebec and Primate of Canada (Roman Catholic)
- The Right Reverend Russel F. Brown, Bishop of Quebec (Anglican)
- The Very Reverend Neophytos Spyros (Greek Orthodox)
- The Reverend Edward Bragg (Presbyterian)
- The Reverend Cyril Stewart Cook (United Church)
- The Very Reverend Arthur Coleman, Dean of Quebec (Anglican)

OPPOSITE: Canadians seemed indifferent at first to celebrations to mark the Centennial. In time, a top-down celebration organized by government was matched by spontaneous, bottom-up projects by ordinary Canadians. *Photo: Library and Archives Canada*

The Confederation Train departs Vancouver under grey skies early in its long, transcontinental trek. The train brought Canada's story to the people with innovative displays complete with light and sound features. *Photo: City of Vancouver Archives*

In the coming months, the criticisms would not end, though they would come to be hard to hear over the praise.

Confederation Train

They stood in line by the hundreds and thousands. They stood in orderly, snaking lines from Victoria to Halifax, enduring snow, rain, sleet, unrelenting sun and draining humidity. They waited patiently to explore a mobile museum on steel wheels.

The Confederation Train made a milk run across Canada from west to east, with stops in sixty-three cities in nine provinces. (The train had to skip Newfoundland, with its narrow-gauge railway.) The diesel engine was painted a garish purple, with a white centennial symbol prominent on the nose, below the light. The exterior facades of the coaches were walled in purple-and-white livery featuring the years "1867" and "1967." The locomotive's horns played the first four notes of "O Canada."

"Canada is coming to you! Are you ready?" asked the newspaper advertisements that preceded the train's arrival. "Get ready! Canada's coming to you!"

The people were ready. They came in droves.

Pauline Vanier, vice-regal consort of the ailing governor general, dedicated the train on New Year's Day in Ottawa. "This train is a tribute to Canadian achievement. It brings attention to the past and will provide inspiration for the future," she said. "We achieved physical unity in the last hundred years . . . we must strive for spiritual unity in the second century." The train then pulled out of the station, bound for Victoria.

More than seventy thousand people boarded the train in British Columbia. Once on board, they wound through displays that told Canada's story from the ice age to Centennial Year, in displays including light and sound effects. The depiction of steerage-class travel in a colonial ship was particularly harrowing: the space dark and claustrophobic, the sound system playing wailing babies and tubercular coughs. Also on display were primeval forests and darkened mine shafts, Great War trenches and a Chamber of Confederation dedicated to the meetings that led to the nation's formation.

The six exhibition coaches featured more than a hundred relics on loan from museums and private collections, including planking from Jacques Cartier's ship, Louis Riel's pistol, Joseph Howe's printing press, Sitting Bull's beaded rifle case, a 1929 stock ticker, a twelfth-century Viking sword, and the rusted anchor from Arctic explorer Roald Amundsen's ship *Gjøa*.

The train had two engines, six exhibition coaches and another seven service cars with sleeping, dining and baggage facilities for the twenty-six-men crews, including electricians, mechanics and exhibit attendants. The RCMP also provided a seven-man security contingent.

The coaches were usually open for at least twelve hours every day, and for fourteen at some stops. There was no admission charge. About eight thousand viewers could get through the exhibition in a day.

Musician Bobby Gimby rode the rails, playing his hit song, "Canada," at each stop on the route.

In Brandon, Manitoba, people waited up to five hours for their tour, which could last from forty-five minutes to an hour. In Kenora, the millionth guest

Train Horns Play on

After 1967, the Confederation Train's horns wound up atop the BC Hydro Building in Vancouver, where they sounded every day at noon. After that building was converted into a condominium, the horns went into storage before being installed at Canada Place in 1994, where they are heard to this day.

MUSICAL ENGINEER ROBERT SWANSON

At noon every day, horns sound from atop Canada Place on the Vancouver waterfront. Ten horns sound the four opening notes of "O Canada" at 115 decibels. They were designed by Robert Swanson, an engineer and sound specialist, who originally built them for the Confederation Train. *Photo: James Stewart / Flickr*

The Confederation Train's whistle of "O Canada"—replicated by the caravans—was the creation of Robert Swanson, chief engineer for British Columbia's Department of Transport. He modified the mandatory crossing warning of two longs, a short and a long to sound like the opening notes of the national anthem. He changed the first blast from an E flat minor to a major and added two aluminum horns to provide bass octaves.

Swanson was born in England and came to Canada prior to the outbreak of World War I. He got his first job repairing boilers at the Jingle Pot coal mine on Vancouver Island, before repairing steam donkeys in the woods for loggers, at age fourteen. He later managed to qualify for an engineering degree without ever having attended a university class.

He developed a fail-safe air braking system for logging trucks and, later, devised a hexatone airhorn assembly for diesel trains, which became the industry standard.

Swanson also wanted to be a writer and sent copies of his gold-rush prose to his favourite poet, Robert Service, the Bard of the Yukon. They later met at Service's brother's bookstore in Vancouver, where the Yukon poet urged him to write not about a land he had never visited but about the woods in which he worked. Swanson became a best-selling poet; his chapbooks included *Rhymes of a Western Logger, Rhymes of a Lumberjack, Rhymes of a Haywire Hooker* and *Bunkhouse Ballads*.

Long lines marked the stops for the Confederation Train. School children were taken on class trips to see the mobile museum by the tens of thousands. *Photo: Library and Archives Canada*

boarded the train shortly after Premier John Robarts welcomed it to Ontario. The train arrived in Ottawa for Dominion Day; some 113,837 visitors passed through the cars during its twelve-day stay.

An astonishing crowd of twenty thousand waited patiently on the grounds of the Canadian National Exhibition in Toronto, where they were entertained by such acts as a steel band from the West Indies.

At Jean Talon Station in north-end Montreal, a protest by seventy separatist demonstrators overwhelmed the RCMP officers on hand. The protesters broke exterior lights and splashed yellow and black paint on the coaches. The train's assistant manager blamed the Montreal police for their slow response to the hostile crowd; the city police intervened after one enraged protester knocked a red-coated Mountie to the ground.

Altogether, 2,739,700 visitors viewed the train's exhibits, almost three times as many as had been expected.

A girl checks out the bowler hat worn by a mannequin of a dandy panning for gold in the Yukon. The display was among the historical exhibits in the travelling Centennial Caravan, which visited smaller communities out of reach of the Centennial Train.
Photo: Dick Darrell / Toronto Star

CONFEDERATION CARAVANS CALLED IN

To reach communities not accessible by the Confederation Train, eight caravans of eight trucks each stopped at nearly seven hundred cities, towns and hamlets. They rolled as far north as Fort Rae in the Northwest Territories and as far east as the Labrador town of Wabash, Newfoundland. The caravans contained displays similar to those on the Train, including a sandbagged trench from World War I and a city slicker in a bowler hat, haplessly panning for gold in the Klondike.

The "history book on wheels" made regional tours, finally stopping at the Grey Cup game in Ottawa. The caravans drew more than seven million visitors, roughly double the projected amount. The trucks were the largest vehicles on North American highways that year.

Centennial Symbol

Graphic designer Stuart Ash was working for the Toronto firm Cooper & Beatty Limited when the commission to design a celebratory logo for the Centennial Commission came into the office. Ash got the assignment. He retreated to his cubicle and, in short order, sketched out a stylized maple leaf. The rough drawing was shown to design director Anthony Mann, his mentor. "Well, what about this?" Ash asked.

"That's it!" Mann responded.

The final version depicted a multi-coloured maple leaf consisting of eleven equilateral triangles, representing the ten provinces and the northern territories. The image was immediately recognizable and was simple enough for a child with crayons and scissors to recreate alongside classmates.

Soon, the image was ubiquitous throughout the land. It appeared on postage stamps and on dollar bills, on enamel lapel pins and on silver centennial medals. On flags, it flew at the North Pole and on Parliament Hill. The symbol was illuminated in electric light on the face of Queen's Park in Toronto and painted in white on the nose of the purple Confederation Train.

"It was planted in flowerbeds," Ash said, "stencilled into concrete sidewalks, and I even recall it being tattooed and cut into people's hair."

It also was stamped, engraved and imprinted on all manner of souvenirs, kitchenware, jewellery and kitsch.

Ash's symbol anticipated the maple leaf on the new Canadian flag, which had yet to have its formal first appearance when Centennial Commission Chairman John Fisher unveiled Ash's creation in January 1965.

Back in 1964, the federal government had offered a first prize of $2,500 when announcing a competition open to all Canadian designers for an official centennial symbol. The government recommended that the designs incorporate the numerals "1867-1967," "67" or "100" and be understandable in both English and French, declaring an automatic disqualification for any design that wasn't bilingual.

The contest drew 496 entries, 307 of which incorporated the maple leaf. The three top finishers earned cash awards, though their designs were rejected. One, using two doves of peace, resembled the trademark of a paper company; another, with concentric "C"s, was similar to that of a can company; while the third, featuring an open "C" embracing ten stars, looked like the familiar logo of a meat-packing firm.

In Ash's words, all were "banal, predictable or clichéd." So, the government settled on a design firm, and hit a "bingo" with Ash.

The *Toronto Star* took Ash's new design to the streets for a reaction. "Confused," the newspaper quoted sales promoter Marg Jacques as saying. "If it is supposed to be a maple leaf, let it look like one and not some kind of puzzle." Manufacturer's agent Paul Valliquette said he was not inspired by the logo. "Shouldn't inspiration be the purpose of such an important symbol? It is too geometrical to be warm and stirring." Blanche Meechin, an exhibitor, thought it looked like a Star of David and would upset Arabs in Canada. Vern Baker, a salesman, said, "It is not imaginative, exciting or attractive. Whatever it is, it definitely isn't obvious. If it is to mean anything to me or to the rest of Canadians, it should be something symbolic of Confederation."

The Commission placed advertisements in newspapers across the land to introduce the work and to encourage its use. "This is the Centennial Symbol," the ads stated. "What does it mean? What does it mean to you?" Readers could send away to the Centennial Commission—at P.O. Box 1967, Ottawa—for a free manual on the use of the Centennial Symbol: "We'd like you to use the symbol in your home; your office; at school; in your plant; wherever you can . . . Let's all be a symbol for Canada, the same way this is a symbol for Centennial."

Perhaps the most widespread use of the symbol came from Salada Foods, which included the stylized maple leaf on all its food lines, including instant mashed potatoes, desserts, marmalades, snack foods and orange juice. The decision meant that the logo would also appear on a billion—count 'em, 1,000,000,000—tea-bag tags sold in the United States. The tags, attached to the tea bags by a thin string, carried the symbol with the words, "Visit Canada—Centennial Year 1967."

Despite the public's early resistance, the symbol was a tremendous success and was much applauded within the design community. Ash, who later designed a memorable mark for the Metric Commission—featuring another stylized maple leaf nestled within the letter "M"—formed the Gottschalk + Ash firm, which went on to challenge the world's top design companies.

In 2014, the federal government repeated its 1964 mistake, once again announcing a speculative logo contest. "Fifty years ago a logo contest did not yield the desired results," Ash said. "I believe that the approach by the government to our sesquicentennial in 2017 does not address Canada's stature

OPPOSITE: The print advertising campaign by the Centennial Commission, run by Vickers and Benson, showed some *Mad Men*-era genius. The centennial symbol, designed by Stuart Ash, was so simple a child could draw it—and many did. The commission wanted the image spread as far as possible. Fifty years later, you can still find the symbol carved into concrete across the land. *Photo: Library and Archives Canada*

Take this Centennial Symbol

Put it on a banner, use it on your products, and in your advertising, engrave it on your stationery, paint it on your vehicles, wear it on your lapel, display it on your cartons, hang it in your plant or office, stick it on your pay envelopes, stencil it on your coffee cups. Carry it. Fly it. But above all

Use it.

THE CENTENNIAL

The new Canadian maple-leaf flag was not yet three years old when it was used to decorate a centennial medallion. The flip side included the ubiquitous centennial symbol.
Photo: woody1778a / Flickr

and sophistication [as] a world-class society and global leader."

Ariana Cuvin, a University of Waterloo student, won the contest and a five-thousand-dollar prize for her design incorporating diamond shapes into a stylized maple leaf representing Canada's ten provinces and three territories. The winning design was heavily criticized—Ash himself called it "complicated, confusing"—though remarks were tempered so as not to pillory a student designer.

In a news release, Adrian Jean, president of the Graphic Designers of Canada, said, "The government's contest exploits a student's drive for exposure and recognition, then wraps it up in the Canadian flag and says it's good for students? That's not fair and that's not how you do business in 2014."

Money, Medals and Medallions

ALEX COLVILLE'S COINS

Canadians can be a crotchety bunch, finding fault in everything. We complain about the loss of tradition, act suspicious of change, and challenge those we suspect of thinking well of themselves. The Canadian ethos may well have been captured in the title of Alice Munro's short story collection *Who Do You Think You Are?*

When the Royal Canadian Mint rolled out commemorative coins for Centennial Year, with the first design changes to the reverse in thirty years, some were offended by the alteration. The coins depicted Canadian wildlife, with a fish replacing the venerated Bluenose schooner and a bunny bumping the beaver. What possible connection was there between these critters and the historical significance of Confederation?

D.R. Barker wrote a letter to the editor of the *Ottawa Journal* complaining that the new coins showed "the dullest array of designs." Why use animals also common in the United States, he groused. Why depict them realistically, he grumped. Why not show scenes depicting historical events, or regional scenes, or indigenous art?

A Nebraska numismatist cheekily declared the coins to be "a veritable Orwellian animal farm."

The reverses of the six new coins featured a soaring dove on the penny, a running rabbit on the nickel, a mackerel on the dime, a prowling wildcat on the quarter, a howling wolf on the half-dollar, and a flapping Canada goose on the silver dollar.

The designs were commissioned by an eleven-member board of judges, one of whom, incidentally, was the man responsible for creating the Expo 67 logo. "The power and beauty of these designs reflects the character and spirit of our people," Finance Minister Mitchell Sharp said when the images of the coins were released in April 1966. The artist was Alex Colville, the New Brunswick painter known for his hyperrealistic images with implied narratives.

The call for proposals attracted interest from many Canadian artists. By the mid-1960s, Colville had earned a modest worldwide reputation for his art, with one-man shows in New York and London and his works representing Canada at the thirty-third Venice Biennale, though by 1966 he had only held his second solo show in his native land, and that in the basement art gallery of Hart House in Toronto.

Colville was born in Toronto and moved to Amherst, Nova Scotia, as a boy. He graduated in 1942 with a fine arts degree from Mount Allison University in Sackville, New Brunswick. Soon after, he enlisted in the Canadian army, where he rose in the ranks, earning commission as an officer. In 1944, he was dispatched to London as an official war artist, serving in the Mediterranean Theatre, as well as in the Netherlands and northern Germany. Toward war's end, Colville arrived at the liberated Bergen-Belsen concentration camp, where cadavers were scattered like discarded cordwood and the only difference in appearance between the skeletal dead and the skeletal living was that one group was ambulatory, barely. On his return home after the war, he completed haunting paintings of what he had seen.

Colville lived a semi-rural life in Sackville, where he gave up teaching at

Alex Colville enlisted in the infantry in 1942. After two years' service, he was made a war artist. As a painter, he was known for striking, hyperrealistic, almost dream-state imagery. He won a competition to design coins to mark the centenary, producing a memorable commemorative set featuring a rock dove (penny), hare (nickel), mackerel (dime), lynx (quarter), wolf (half-dollar) and Canada goose (dollar). *Photo: Library and Archives Canada*

the university to dedicate himself full-time to art. The designs he submitted for the centennial coins reflected the life he saw on walks in small-town New Brunswick, where there was comfort in the familiar.

"I picked animals because I felt they were appropriate," he told the writer Cyril Robinson of *Weekend Magazine*. "I felt that only animals would provide themes with sufficient depth." As the men walked across a furrowed farm field, Alex's dog in tow, Robinson pressed him for details about the selection of each animal. The rock dove on the penny? "The dove has associations with both peace and spiritual values." The hare on the five-cent piece? "For fertility and new life." The mackerel? "One of the most beautiful fishes of the sea." The lynx? "Formidable and intelligent." The wolf? "Symbolic of the vastness and loneliness of our land." Finally, the goose in full flight on the dollar? "Particularly Canadian and majestic."

Left unstated was the possible influence on Colville of the coins that English sculptor Percy Metcalfe had produced for the Irish Free State in 1928. Those coins included a hare and an Irish wolfhound in spare, precise lines, much as Colville's designs did four decades later. While Metcalfe depicted his creatures on a base, the Canadian's drawings allow the animals to float in the centre of the coin, a flowing placement, especially for the birds. The Canada goose has "a kind of serene dynamic quality," Colville is quoted as saying in the Master of the Mint's annual report.

Colville pronounced himself "gobsmacked" that all six of his designs were selected. Four other artists received honourable mentions, though their designs were not made public. However, two of the runner-up submissions were displayed at a branch of the Royal Trust Company in Toronto as part of a show of currency oddities.

The sculptor Elizabeth Wyn Wood proposed a series of designs known as "Canada Builds," with a tepee on the penny, an igloo on the nickel, a townhouse on the dime, a parish church on the quarter, a wood-burning freight engine on the half-dollar, and a grain elevator and lake freighter on the dollar. (The resident of Willowdale, Ontario, now a neighbourhood in North York, was known for a modernist style in sculpture as well as for monumental public commissions in Ontario such as fountains and war memorials. Wood died shortly after submitting her proposal, at the age of sixty-two.)

Eric Aldwinckle of Toronto envisioned coins showing the bounty of the land with symbols representing trees, water and fish on the five-cent piece. The dime was to carry a wheat sheaf with ten kernels representing the provinces, while the fifty-cent piece had a snow crystal. The dollar had a complicated and busy design with the coats of arms of Canada's ten provinces and two territories surrounding the Canadian Arms. The quarter featured the bust of Sir John A. Macdonald, Canada's first prime minister.

The other also-rans were Rolan Guilbault of Jonquiere, Quebec, and Arthur Price of Cyrville, Ontario. Each of the four received an award of $3,000 for their rejected designs. Colville was given $9,000 for his designs, which is a lot of mackerels. (That's about $63,500 in today's dollars.)

At the time, Colville was completing only about three paintings per year and his works were not as widely known as they would become. Then, in one year, his works were in every Canadian's hands.

The obverse of the centennial coins featured Arnold Machin's portrait of a right-facing bust of a young Queen Elizabeth wearing a jewel-studded tiara and drapery on her shoulder, an image introduced in 1965 and remaining on all Canadian coins until 1989. Her image was flanked by the words "QUEEN ELIZABETH II D.G. REGINA," the initials standing for the Latin "*Dei Gratia*" ("by the grace of God") and "*Regina*" meaning "the Queen." The reverse of the Colville coins included the denomination above the animal, with the legend "CANADA 1867–1967" below.

The centennial coinage was produced in massive numbers with a mintage of four million half-dollars, more than six million dollars, forty-eight million quarters and sixty-three million dimes. The Mint returned the following year to its regular designs of one-cent maple leaves, five-cent beavers, twenty-five-cent caribous, and voyageurs in a canoe on the dollar coins.

Through his work, Colville sought an everlasting existence unavailable to a mere mortal. "Art tries to compensate for the lack of permanence in life," he once said. A half-century later, the coins he designed are regarded as some of the most beautiful ever minted. To this day, they occasionally appear among your change, worthy of a moment's reflection and a happy reminder of an exciting year: hand-held sculptures that put art into the pocket of even the poorest.

GOLD COINS

Finance Minister Mitchell Sharp heaved on a starting lever, causing a ninety-ton press to strike the first gold coin issued by Canada in more than a half-century. The size of a quarter, the twenty-dollar gold coin had an effigy of the Queen on the face and the Canadian coat of arms on the reverse.

Some 1967 Canadian dollar bills replaced serial numbers with the centenary years of 1867 and 1967. *Photo: Bank of Canada Museum*

Banknote adjustment

The Canadian one-dollar banknote was modified for the Centennial. A view of the original Parliament Buildings—destroyed by fire in 1916—replaced a prairie landscape on the back. On the face, a centennial symbol was added, and the dates 1867 and 1967 appeared instead of the serial number.

The Royal Canadian Mint marketed a special presentation package of the seven centennial coins. They were placed in silk-lined cases of morocco leather processed in England—a suitable, high-class nest for a gold coin, four silver coins, a coin of nickel and a copper penny. Canada had last issued five-dollar and ten-dollar gold coins in 1914. The nation was off the Gold Standard, so gold coins were not produced for general circulation, although the Mint had to accept that some of the coins included in presentation sets could be used in regular commerce. While the face value of the coins was $21.91, the package sold for $40 (about $280 in today's money). The Mint spent $35 to produce the boxed set, the cases alone costing about $4 each. The exterior of the case bore the Canadian coat of arms.

The Mint expected to sell between thirty thousand and forty thousand of the special presentation sets. By August of 1967, it had received orders for more than a quarter-million sets. They announced that orders would no longer be taken after September, and another one hundred thousand requests came in. The backlog was not filled until the following summer.

Today, these sets sell for about eight hundred dollars, a reflection of the inflated value of the gold in the twenty-dollar coin. The Mint also marketed twelve-dollar sets, with the gold coin replaced by a silver medallion, and four-dollar sets of the six common coins sealed in plastic packages.

The government and Expo 67 officials presented the sets with gold coins as gifts to heads of state and visiting royalty.

"We don't have many gifts that are distinctively Canadian, but this is one," said N.A. Parker, Master of the Mint. "Besides, the twenty-dollar piece is a beautiful coin."

CENTENNIAL MEDALS GALORE

Marie Callahan arrived for work at Parliament Hill before dawn on a November morning in 1967 in Ottawa, as she had done for twenty-seven years.

She had taken the job after the untimely death of her husband. With a young daughter to support, the widow had been fortunate to find work cleaning Centre Block. Her day began at five a.m., when she set about scrubbing rest rooms and preparing towels for the use of members of Parliament and their secretaries. The early start allowed her to be home for her daughter after school. She had not missed a day of work in seven years.

On this morning, the sixty-three-year-old cleaner brought with her a small item that had arrived in the mail. A friend pinned it to her chest and she wore it proudly throughout the work day, "although I think it's supposed to be for ceremonial occasions."

That morning, John Diefenbaker, who earlier that year had lost his position as Opposition leader, spotted the silver disk. "Mr. Diefenbaker congratulated me this morning and said I had certainly been an honest, faithful person while serving him," she told the *Ottawa Journal*.

Marie was one of 29,500 Canadians to receive a Centennial Medal, a circular silver medal with a thin raised rim. The obverse displays the Royal cypher ("ERII") superimposed on a maple leaf surrounded by the legend "CONFEDERATION CANADA CONFÉDÉRATION." The reverse includes the Canadian coat of arms and the dates 1867–1967. The medal was to be worn on a white ribbon with red edges and thin red stripes.

As an honour, the Centennial Medal followed in the Order of Precedence the medals for valour, war service and military decorations, but came before those awarded for long service or good conduct.

A medal was mailed to Louise Card, national president of the Business and Professional Women's Clubs of Canada, in Neepawa, Manitoba. Another arrived for Nelson Shoemaker, the Liberal who represented the constituency of Gladstone-Neepawa in the provincial legislature. The letter from the Office of the Secretary of State said the honour was "in recognition of valuable service to the nation."

In Coqualeetza, a farming community in British Columbia's Fraser Valley, a medal was presented to Mary Malloway, who was said to have been born in the district in 1857, a year before the Fraser gold rush and a decade before

Testing, Testing...

On October 1, 1968, five men began the rituals necessary to complete a medieval tradition known as the Trial of the Pyx. The pyx is the traditional box for storing coins to be tested for purity.

The government scientists—two from the National Research Council, three from the Department of Energy, Mines and Resources—had been sworn in as the Assay Commission Board by a county court judge in Ottawa. The scientists were responsible for testing the centennial twenty-dollar gold coin and the commemorative silver issue.

In Canada, the assay was a sixty-year tradition required by law, to ascertain that the coins held the correct amount of precious metals as determined by government regulation. The five conducted chemical and metallurgical tests on coins selected at random from every forty-five-pound bag of coins produced by the Mint.

With gold coins issued only for special occasions, and nickel replacing silver in Canadian coins, it was thought that the centennial testing would be the last annual Trial of the Pyx.

About 29,500 Canadian Centennial Medals were issued, with more than eight thousand going to Canadian Forces personnel. So many medals were struck by the Canadian Mint, and so disorganized was the distribution, that the program suffered embarrassments, including the auctioning of medals by a service group. Many who got one were grateful, including Parliament Hill charwoman Marie Callahan, who was honoured for twenty-seven years' service. *Photo: Canadian Museum of History*

Confederation. At the nearby Canadian Forces Base Chilliwack, Col. R.W. Potts handed out twenty-three medals at parade. The recipients included eight wireless operators, five corporals, three sergeants, a captain, a lieutenant, a band sergeant, a fire captain, a private and two civilians.

At Brandon, Manitoba, the Queen's cousin, Princess Alexandra, presented medals to a baker's dozen of students from kindergarten to Grade 12.

The prime minister handed out twenty-three medals to young players competing at the Canadian Centennial Junior Tennis Championship at the Rideau Lawn Tennis Club.

Roy Greenaway, a seventy-six-year-old retired correspondent for the *Toronto Star*, whose biggest scoop had been about the discovery of insulin, got a medal in the mail.

A medal even arrived on remote Graham Island, largest of the Queen

Charlottes, now known as Haida Gwaii, off the windswept northern coast of British Columbia. It was for thirty-nine-year-old Mrs. Arnold Peterson of Skidegate, a mother of eleven, who had become the first indigenous person elected as a school trustee in the province. (In keeping with newspaper conventions of the time, her given first name was not included in press accounts.) She had attended a day school for native students, a pedagogical approach she decried as unacceptable as Canada entered its second century.

"It was all right for our time," she said, adding:

> We learned to read and write so we could get along. But we could not get beyond Grade 8. There was nothing here for anyone passing the entrance exams. Some students were through Grade 8 twice because they were too young to quit school and had nowhere to take high school. Today, things are different. Native children have every opportunity. Under the provincial system, children are able to advance more quickly and there are improvements.

RECIPIENTS ON THE SEPARATIST FRONT

Despite the many worthy recipients of Centennial Medals, the sheer number of honours soon brought the entire exercise into disrepute. Recipients included:

- René Lévesque, then an independent member of Quebec's National Assembly, who wrote in his column in the weekly newspaper *Dimanche-Matin* that he'd received a medal from the secretary of state for "service to Canada," the very nation from which he wished independence. One letter-writer to the *Toronto Star*—undoubtedly still smarting from French President Charles De Gaulle's cry of "Vive le Québec libre!"—suggested that Lévesque was more deserving of the Croix de Guerre.
- Gilles Grégoire, who sat in the House of Commons as an independent though he was a leader of the separatist Ralliement nationale party. He wore his centennial medal on his lapel when he attended a separatist rally in Quebec City, saying he was going to auction the medal to raise money for his cause.

Among other news, more than a third of the medals went to armed forces personnel, most of them commissioned officers, or brass in military jargon. Another eight hundred were distributed to federal and provincial legislators.

A few years after Marie Callahan received her honour, a magazine writer found her still at work in Centre Block, where she'd been assigned to lighter duties, such as dusting the Opposition lobby. She missed her old job and found the new one dull. "On the towels it was different; you got the run of the whole building," she said. She also missed the daily interaction with politicians, when a cleaning lady could converse with a former prime minister with whom she shared a workplace—as well as an honour bestowed in the Queen's name.

OVERTIME AT THE MINT

The Mint worked overtime to keep up with demand in 1967. Hundreds of millions of commemorative centennial coins were struck, as were more than five million medallions. As well, the Mint delivered 5,001 nickel coins ordered by the government of the Northwest Territories. Those were to be delivered to the families of every child born in the territories during the year.

Among the private orders for medals the Mint fulfilled during the year included commissions from the Royal Bank of Canada, the Engineering Institute of Canada, the Department of Transport, the Royal Canadian Geographical Society and the Professional Institute of the Public Service of Canada. The National Film Board ordered ten silver medals for photographic excellence. Finally, the Royal Society of Canada put in a modest order for just two medals, though those were made of eighteen-karat gold.

The Alberta town of Provost issued a token to mark the nation's centennial. The reverse carried an image of the local school, while the obverse displayed a grain elevator. Many communities across Canada issued coins and tokens to mark the birthday. *Photo: woody1778a / Flickr*

MILLIONS OF MEDALLIONS

School children usually go home at the end of classes with homework. On June 1, 1967, they also had souvenirs in hand, as schools distributed a brass medallion to each of the millions of students, as a centennial keepsake. The Canada Confederation Medal came wrapped in a cellophane package, which many children immediately tore open to get at the prize inside.

The Royal Canadian Mint produced 5,623,923 brass medallions. The face showed the Crown atop the Shield of Canada, which includes the royal symbols of Britain and France, from the three royal lions of England and the royal lion of Scotland, as well as a trio of royal fleur-de-lys from France and the royal Irish harp of Tara. Three maple leaves at the base represent Canadian diversity. The medallion's obverse includes the stylized maple leaf of the centennial symbol, the triangles featuring diagonal stripes.

A slightly larger medallion in silver was distributed by the Department of Secretary of State. The Mint made 29,500 of those.

The obverse was designed by Thomas Shingles, the Mint's former master engraver, who had moved to British Columbia. The reverse was created by the Toronto's Dora de Pédery-Hunt, a Hungarian-born sculptor who would later design the gold coin for the 1976 Olympics in Montreal. Each design was worth $1,500 for the creator.

Centennial Rose

The first salvo in Canada's "War of the Roses" was fired at the Canadian Nursery Trades Association's annual convention in 1964. On display in Winnipeg was a striking pink-and-cream flower developed by Fred Blakeney, an octogenarian grower from Victoria, BC. At the convention, delegates voted to name the rose 'Miss Canada'; it was to be their submission as the official rose of the Centennial.

The nurserymen were opposing a rival bid by the Rotary Clubs in Canada, which were running a contest of their own to select an official centennial rose. All Rotary contenders were American varieties, which the native nurserymen called "absolutely silly."

"The nurserymen's rose is born and bred in Canada," president Len Cullen said of the 'Miss Canada' bloom. "We do not think Canada should have an imported American rose for her Centennial."

Montreal businessman Jack McIntyre, a rose grower by hobby, led the Rotary Club effort. A selection panel chose three unnamed top test blooms, which were then planted in twenty test gardens. More than eighteen thousand gardening enthusiasts chose their favourite, an orange-red flower.

The Canadian Centennial Rose decorates an English-made bone china teacup and saucer. *Photo: Natale Ghent*

The thorny dispute was settled when the Centennial Commission, under John Fisher, anointed the Rotary rose as the officially designated rose. It was registered and trademarked as the Canadian Centennial Rose.

When the Queen donated $25,000 to a Quebec charity for developmentally disabled children, a cause the Rotarians supported, they sent five hundred Centennial Roses to Buckingham Palace as thanks. The rose also found its way into royal houses at Sandringham and Balmoral, as well as into the Royal Horticultural Society's Garden at Wisley, in Surrey. Centennial Rose bushes were planted at the International Peace Garden that straddles the forty-ninth parallel on the Manitoba–North Dakota border. Ten thousand were planted on the grounds of Expo 67.

A non-profit foundation was formed to ensure that proceeds from the sales of the official rose went to charity. "Planting the Centennial Rose commemorates our past, it beautifies our present living, and the cause for which it works contributes to our future," McIntyre said.

A vibrant fluorescence of coral with a soft salmon overtone gave the Centennial Rose a distinctive look on its release in 1966, in time for blooms in Centennial Year. A.V. Stanton, the garden editor at the *Ottawa Journal*, encouraged readers to plant the rose along house foundations or along driveways. "It doesn't grow more than two feet high," he wrote, "so will look well around a bird bath, flagpole, statuary, in the corner of the patio—in fact, anywhere you have a square foot of earth."

Stanton also had praise for its rival in the "War of the Roses," saying that the striking 'Miss Canada' was best for bouquets and arrangements.

The 'Miss Canada' was hybridized by Blakeney, a British Columbia rose grower, formerly from Ottawa, who lived on a city lot on the Gorge Waterway, a saltwater inlet connected to Victoria's Inner Harbour. The flower was distributed by H.M. Eddie & Sons Limited of Vancouver, which offered the following description: "The parentage is Peace and Karl Herbst, which have produced this lusty grower with strong, thick stems. It is an almost continuous bloomer of beautiful pink-blend rose madder and silver reverse. Foliage is thick and leathery." The nicely perfumed rose bushes sold at $2.75 each, or three for $7.50.

Reviews of 'Miss Canada' in the *Canadian Rose Annual* were mixed, though most praised the hardiness of the plant. One grower pronounced himself satisfied with the attractiveness of the blooms—"but what an array of thorns which stand on guard."

The two contenders vied with the Confederation Rose, distributed by Ellesmere Nursery, a pink rose bred by Adam Golik in 1964 on the hundredth anniversary of the Charlottetown Conference, which had led to Confederation.

As well as the 'Miss Canada' rose, the nurseryman designated another favoured centennial plant: the 'Almey Crabapple'. Named for the horticulturalist J.R. Almey, it was developed and introduced in 1945 at the Morden Experimental Station, south of Winnipeg. Almey chose it from among 1,700 seedlings in flower at the time. The crabapple is known for large purple flowers with a white marking at the base of each petal. Meanwhile, the Ontario Horticultural Association designated a centennial crabapple of its own. 'The Royalty,' known

ROSe BUSH OR THE PLAGUe?

A centennial committee that published a newsletter containing a list of suggested projects for the residents of Brandon, Manitoba, received more publicity than expected.

For one dollar, a refugee child could be fed for a month, the newsletter said, while two dollars bought a blanket for the child. A 'Miss Canada' rose bush could be purchased for $2.75. "Ten dollars," the newsletter stated, "will mark a local historic site with a plague."

The typographical error tickled the funny bones of the editorial writers at the *Brandon Sun*, who wrote:

"Now who would want to do a thing like that? It reminds us of a recent dispute between two homeowners, both of whom claimed to reside in a house once occupied by Sir John A. Macdonald. The man from the historical society listened less and less patiently as the two men argued over whose house should be marked as a historical site. Finally he could take it no longer. 'A plaque on both your houses!' he said."

for its glossy, dark reddish-purple foliage and resistance to disease, originated in Sutherland, Saskatchewan.

Some smaller Canadian cities adopted programs to blanket their parks and boulevards with selected plants. In Ontario, Morrisburg went with lilacs, while Brockville chose the beautybush. In Peterborough, a tulip bed was planted in the shape of the new Canadian flag.

The Dutch Bulb Growers spent two years developing a tulip capable of thriving in the soil and climate conditions found in all ten provinces. The tulips, which produced large, brilliant red flowers, were the focus of a fundraising campaign by the Canadian Cystic Fibrosis Foundation. A basket of bulbs was delivered to Secretary of State Judy LaMarsh on Parliament Hill one September morning in 1966, the start of a million-bulb blitz across the land. Some of those centennial tulips would bloom again the following year, at about the same time that a novelty falsetto singer named Tiny Tim hit the record charts with "Tip-Toe Thru' the Tulips."

Centennial Tartan–for Go-Go Dresses, Too

Several different tartans were celebrated during Centennial Year:

Canadian Centennial Tartan: This tartan featured six colours: blue, green, yellow and black to represent natural resources, with red and white representing the national flag. The design is credited to a Scottish designer, though the tartan was marketed as the Centennial Tartan by brothers Harold and Henry Weller, who got approval for the name from the Centennial Commission. The tartan appeared on a wide variety of items, including swimsuits and go-go dresses.

British Columbia Tartan: The Pacific province commissioned its own tartan to celebrate the Centennial. Designed by Earl Kitchener Ward of Langford, a Victoria suburb, the tartan was coloured blue (symbolizing the Pacific Ocean), gold (the Crown), white (Dogwood, the provincial flower), red (the maple leaf) and green (forests). This was officially adopted by the province in 1974.

Yukon Tartan: Janet Couture, a jeweller from Watson Lake, proposed a non-traditional tartan for the territory in 1967. It included blue (signifying the sky), green (forests), white (snow), yellow (gold), magenta (fireweed) and dark blue (mountains and lakes). This was officially adopted by the territory in 1984.

The Centennial Tartan appeared on all manner of clothing for men and women. The blue, green, yellow and black were said to represent Canada's natural resources, while the white and red are the only colours found on the national flag. *Photo: Canadian Museum of History*

Maple Leaf Tartan: David Weiser of Toronto designed a tartan in 1964 in anticipation of the coming centennial. His pattern incorporated green, gold, red and brown threads to mimic the effect of the seasons on a maple leaf. The Queen Mother saw the tartan on display at a private fashion show staged at the Covent Garden Opera House in London, though the pattern was also in such mundane items as automobile throws and seat covers. Bandleader Guy Lombardo and his Royal Canadians wore dinner jackets of the Maple Leaf Tartan for a performance at the New York World's Fair on Dominion Day, 1965. The tartan was also adopted by the Regimental Pipes and Drums of the Royal Canadian Regiment. Forty-seven years after it was introduced, the federal government announced that the Maple Leaf Tartan was Canada's official tartan.

A Typeface for Canada

All Canadians can read about their liberties in the constitutional document known as the Charter of Rights and Freedoms, which is written in language more utilitarian than stirring. That language, dull though it may be, is expressed in a typeface known as Cartier. It was the first Latin typeface designed and cut by a Canadian.

The typeface creator was Carl Dair, a designer without formal art-school training. Born in Welland, Ontario, he worked as a newsboy and salesman for

Carl Dair was commissioned to design the first Canadian typeface in English as a centennial project. He named his elegant typeface Cartier, after the French explorer. Carl Dair's hand-drawn letters were the first Latin typeface designed by a Canadian. The designer Rod McDonald has updated the typeface as Cartier Book for the digital age, introducing the face to a new generation. *Photos: Carl Dair Fonds, Robertson Davies Library, Massey College*

the local newspaper before getting a job designing and laying out advertising for the *Stratford Beacon-Herald*. After moving to Montreal, he became typographical director for the National Film Board and opened a design studio. His *Design With Type* has been a standard text on the subject since its first publication soon after the war. It remains in print.

He continued lecturing and writing about typography after resettling in Toronto. It rankled him that no Canadian typeface had been devised since 1840, when James Evans, a Methodist missionary in what is now Manitoba, created a Cree syllabic that was used in the printing of religious materials, the crude type apparently cast from the lead lining scavenged from tea chests. A government fellowship allowed Dair to travel with his young family to the Netherlands, where he spent a year studying the painstaking techniques employed at the Joh. Enschedéen Zonen type foundry in Haarlem.

In 1957, he began designing a distinctive Canadian typeface for text composition. He devised a novel and elegant sans serif typeface, which he named after the explorer Jacques Cartier. It was released on the first day of Centennial Year as a gift to the Canadian people.

Despite his long labours, Dair had only managed to complete the upper- and lower-case roman and lower-case italic letters, in addition to numerals and some punctuation marks. (Oddly, on an early sheet of typeface characters, he had crossed out a stylized fleur-de-lys and a five-pointed maple leaf, which perhaps at one point he intended for use as dingbats.)

Dair, who had been ill, died on a flight home following a lecture in New York later in 1967. He was fifty-five years old.

Over the years, the Cartier typeface fell out of favour, in part because it had not been adapted for use in modern technologies. As well, Dair's design needed refinement to be successful as text as opposed to display lettering. Canadian typographer Rod McDonald revived the face for use in digital reproduction, altering original stroke angles to strengthen the type's horizontal flow. The Cartier Book font family—regular, medium, bold and italic—ensures the continued life of this distinctively Canadian design.

Centennial Café

Sam Young, an immigrant from China, was working in a Vancouver lumberyard when his father told him about a friend opening a restaurant in Medicine Hat, Alberta. "Why don't you go learn the restaurant business," his father said, "and maybe you can open your own one day."

The twenty-one-year-old arrived broke, but eager. The owner of the New Club Café put him to work in the kitchen.

"It was really hot in the kitchen and the other cooks were busy and would get mad all the time, but in all those years I never got mad," Young said. In time, he got a nickname: they called him "Happy. "

After three years, he had saved enough to take over Hi-way Lunch & Confectionary. In 1967, he purchased the New Club Café, at 638 2nd St. S.E., renaming it the Centennial Café. He added a projecting canopy with the café's name and the promise of "Chinese foods." A striking cedar-beam facia stretched to cover the building's second storey, with the centennial logo front and centre.

The owner served free coffee and cake to celebrate the re-opening on May 11. Young sold the restaurant to Greek immigrants three years later. The name and menu were changed. Young managed other restaurants before opening Happy's Family Restaurant. He retired in 2008.

A Centennial Menu

A thirteen-course Centennial Menu was presented to six hundred restaurateurs attending the annual Canadian Restaurant Association show in Toronto. While the show was held in the Automotive Building on the Exhibition Grounds, the feast was served at the Royal York Hotel under the guidance of chef Marcel Didier.

The menu, devised by a committee of cooks and restaurant owners, was designed to span a century of Canadian cuisine, while also featuring foods from the dairies, wheat lands and fishing grounds across the country.

The menu struck some as uninspiring. "It reads a bit as if it all boils down to plain old roast beef and blueberry pie," wrote one critic, "but then, the chefs have fancied it up a bit."

Later in the year, restaurant association president C.C. (Gus) Boukydis went on a twenty-seven-city cross-Canada tour. He acknowledged our country's world-renowned delicacies—citing Arctic char, Winnipeg Goldeye and cheddar cheese—but said foreigners expected one dish in particular. "Canada is known as a country of good beef, even though we think of it as an American speciality," he said. Tastes were changing. "New ethnic restaurants [that] have appeared since the war have enlarged the taste buds of Canadians, and they are becoming more discriminating diners."

Italian, Greek and Chinese restaurants would soon be joined by so many more.

THE ORIGINAL 13-course menu

Pea soup
(QUEBEC)

Hot apple cider flavoured with cloves and cinnamon sticks and served in stone crocks
(NOVA SCOTIA)

Lettuce with a sour cream-maple syrup dressing
(ONTARIO)

Smoked and garnished Atlantic salmon
(NEWFOUNDLAND)

Escalloped potatoes
(PRINCE EDWARD ISLAND)

Green beans with tossed pearl onions and pimentos
(NEW BRUNSWICK)

Roast beef
(ALBERTA)

Preserves, dill pickles, pickled red cabbage, spiced apple rings
(BRITISH COLUMBIA)

Buttermilk tea biscuits
(SASKATCHEWAN)

Blueberry torte with chocolate sauce
(MANITOBA)

Cheddar cheese
(ONTARIO)

The coffee was from Brazil

3

100 Years of Gratitude

Canadians Take Up Challenge with Gusto

FOR THE YEARS leading to 1967, the public seemed indifferent to the pending anniversary. The call from the Centennial Commission for every Canadian to explore the meaning of the nation and its birthday in their own way seemed likely to be as ignored as any other government plea. Let the university eggheads and big-city elites make a big deal about Confederation. Regular Canadians were struggling to put groceries on the table.

In the first week of Centennial Year, *Montreal Gazette* cartoonist John Collins shrugged an Everyman's weary sigh at the call for Canadians to take up a centennial project. He drew an image of canoeists and mountain climbers chasing their ambitious goals, while his poor, barrel-wearing character, Uno Who, flees from traffic, taxes, strikes and the cost of living.

In the end, celebration triumphed over cynicism, and the desire to explore, to achieve and to memorialize inspired legions of Canadians of all ages to make 1967 special. Local newspapers covered these exploits, from the modest (collecting driftwood) to the goofy (an ocean race in bathtubs) to the epic (walking the breadth of Canada). A hitherto quiet people found a voice.

"What can I do for Centennial?" Knit a sweater, Travel Canada, Plant a tree.

The Centennial Commission, led by "Mr. Canada" John Fisher, encouraged everyday Canadians to take up a project to mark the centenary. At first cool to the idea, Canadians eventually embraced it with fervour. *Photo: Library and Archives Canada*

Projects on Land

CROSSING CANADA: HANK GALLANT

Hank Gallant left his home to find work. The choices in his native Prince Edward Island were limited—so, like so many Maritimers before him, he headed west to find fortune, or at least a steady job with a good paycheque. A slight but strong man, who made up for what he lacked in muscular bulk with determination, he laboured in mines in British Columbia. The work was gruelling. He figured that if he added to his skills, he could make more money with less physically demanding work.

Gallant studied welding and learned to operate heavy equipment at a vocational school in Prince George. Both sounded superior to lifting, and certainly promised more pay. Like so many other young people in the heady early days of 1967, twenty-four-year-old Gallant became inspired to undertake a project to mark the Centennial. Low on funds, but armed with a determination that saw him building dams in remote locations with poor weather, the workman settled on a grim, arduous, nearly impossible task. In part, he was fuelled by a vision, fostered since age six, that he was meant to accomplish a special goal, though the nature of it had yet to be revealed in his imagination. Until Centennial Year.

On February 6, Gallant dipped a toe into the saltwater at the foot of Beacon Hill Park in Victoria. He put his socks back on, laced up his boots, adjusted the heavy pack on his back and took a first step northbound from Mile Zero on Douglas Street, Highway One, a terminus of the Trans-Canada Highway.

He had told friends about his plans. They scoffed. He canvassed businesses and service clubs in Prince George for support. They balked. "They didn't take me serious," he later observed. "So I just stopped telling people."

Off he went walking along the shoulder of the highway. Up and over the Malahat, the scenic but treacherous Vancouver Island route to Nanaimo, where he caught a ferry to the mainland. The boat would be the last vehicle of any kind that he'd take for nine months.

On his back was a pack with a change of clothes, his food supplies (raw hamburger, uncooked eggs, chocolate bars), and a Gibson guitar without a case, which he covered with a flap of canvas. A water canteen swung from his neck with every step. He stuck a crude, hand-written sign on the pack: "VICTORIA TO BONIVISTA, CENTENNIAL 67 WALKER, NO RIDES PLEASE." No one had the heart to tell him that Bonavista was misspelled.

He walked through the outskirts of Vancouver and on into the Fraser Valley until he got as far as the felicitously named town of Hope at the end of the valley, after which lay the land jokingly described as being "beyond Hope." Its mountainous terrain had scattered settlements dividing the coast from the prairies. Passing motorists had no idea who the ambling character was on the side of the road.

On the highway from Hope to Princeton, Gallant trudged along, feeling disconcertingly alone. He hadn't seen a vehicle for hours. He'd learn later that the road had been closed at both ends because of a pending storm, the brunt of which he experienced that night. "There was no traffic, no nuttin'," he recalled. "I slept underneath a tree. I tried to stay awake so I wouldn't fall asleep and freeze to death, eh. I had a hard night. The next morning the sun was out. I dug myself out of the ground, out of the snow pressed neat around the tree, and I

A labourer from Prince Edward Island who worked on dams in British Columbia, Hank Gallant expressed his love for the country by walking across it. He began in Victoria in February and nearly lost his life hiking through the mountains. Gallant worked along the way and wrote folk songs, which he strummed on his guitar. In Ottawa, he was arrested for vagrancy. Despite his tribulations, he made it all the way to St. John's, Newfoundland. *Photo:* The Chilliwack Progress

A child plants a tree near an Ottawa apartment block graced by the centennial symbol. *Photo: Library and Archives Canada*

went up the highway." Sometime after 10 a.m., a plough came down the highway from the other direction. The driver was surprised to see him. Gallant spent the next night in a highway crew work camp.

At one point in his journey, he pulled a leg muscle. A rancher treated him with herbs and liniment, and he kept on trudging. This strange, bespectacled creature gained notice during his slow procession eastward. In Kimberley, a couple served him a spaghetti meal. At Cranbrook, forty people waited on the western edge of town to escort him in.

There would be other uncertain nights. "Going through the Crowsnest Pass, from Cranbrook to Fort Macleod and Pincher Creek, there was a blizzard every day. You couldn't see two feet in front of you." One bad night, "I dug a hole in a haystack and got in there, so I wouldn't freeze."

By then, he'd made a vow to himself: "I would die on the side of the road before I'd give up." He would be a highway hermit, walking alone. "I didn't have anyone walk with me. All along, people would ask and I said, 'No. Either you'd be carrying me or I'd be carrying you.'" For companionship, he'd write songs in his head, or try to get birds to answer his calls.

He crossed into Alberta on the afternoon of March 9. He sewed onto his cap a souvenir cloth patch depicting the BC crest. He planned to do so for each of the provinces he conquered. He had the crests of all ten in his pocket.

In Lethbridge, he talked his way into four days of room and board in exchange for entertaining beer-parlour patrons by playing his guitar. By then, Gallant had just $60 left from his $280 grubstake.

Newspapers along the way charted his slow progress.

In early April, he ambled through Moose Jaw, Saskatchewan. At Oak Lake, Manitoba, west of Brandon, a school principal cancelled all classes so the students could greet the centennial walker. On May 1, after enduring his ninth—and worst—blizzard, at –39C with 80 km/h winds, he arrived in the Manitoba capital, where he told a reporter from the *Winnipeg Free Press*:

I can't offer any Centennial project a thousand bucks. This is what I have to offer as an individual Centennial project. It proves to the outside world that Canadians themselves are doing something about Centennial—not only governments, with their libraries and statues.

Gallant worked for several days at a meat-packing plant in Winnipeg, to replenish his funds. Then he hit the road once again.

On isolated stretches of the Trans-Canada through Northern Ontario, truckers recognized the lonely walker as they made their rounds. Some going in his direction would stop at the next town to buy a meal for him at a diner, instructing the waitress to flag down the man walking along the highway for some grub and a rest. On he went, past Kenora and Thunder Bay, on to Wawa and Marathon (that teasing name), then to Sault Ste. Marie and Sudbury and North Bay to the Ottawa River, where the highway followed the river's southeast course to the nation's capital.

Gallant headed to the Sparks Street Mall, where he took out his guitar and began strumming. The police made him stop and told him to get into the patrol car.

"I said, I'll go down to the station, but I won't go in no paddy wagon. My journey's on foot," he recalled. He explained his journey and the police laughed. In the end, he was not charged with vagrancy; he figured a town that stops you from playing music is not a place to linger. He continued to Montreal, where he was feted at Expo 67.

On he walked. He passed through Fredericton in late September, continuing on through New Brunswick until he got to the ferry terminal at Borden, where he returned to his home province. He walked across the island before catching a ferry back to the mainland, hiking through Nova Scotia to catch another, final, ferry to Newfoundland.

On November 13, the 280th day of his march, and coincidentally his twenty-fifth birthday, Gallant strode toward St. John's, where he remembers being met by a large crowd of schoolchildren. "I went to the harbour," he recalled. "I took off my boots and my socks and did what I had done on the Pacific Coast at Beacon Hill Park: I dipped my toe in the Atlantic, and said, 'That's it.'" The final stretch of the Trans-Canada Highway across Newfoundland had been completed only two years earlier. He was the first person to have walked from one Mile Zero to the other.

Gallant eventually resettled on Prince Edward Island, where he worked as a fisherman. In 1999, he published a book, *The Walk: Ten Million Steps Across*

Canada. He lives in Nail Pond and a few years back donated his boots, his backpack and his cap with the provincial badges to the local Tignish Museum.

When asked what he learned about Canada from his monumental walk, he said: "It's not very small, I can tell you that."

DONKEY RIDING: IDA DEKELVER

When Ida DeKelver set off on foot from her ranch home in an isolated British Columbia valley, she was accompanied by two donkeys, named Jack and Bill. Between them, they carried one hundred and forty pounds of provisions. She planned on riding Bill much of the way.

Her destination was her hometown in Saskatchewan, some fourteen hundred kilometres to the east on the other side of the Rocky Mountains.

On the morning of September 15, 1967, she sent the children off to school before bidding *adieu* to her husband, Emil, who left to carry out chores on their sheep ranch. Four friends were on hand to wish her off. "You'll phone back for someone to pick you up at the end of the first hundred miles," one of them said.

Bill quickly tired from carrying a passenger, so Ida redistributed the load, with the older, lead donkey hauling the bulk. The packs included twenty pounds of oats for the animals, two pairs of shoes, cookies, chocolate bars and two jackets, one of which she had altered from an air-force "teddy bear," a fleece-lined jacket issued to aircrew. A movie camera, a projector, and films in canisters were the heaviest items. DeKelver had been unable to get the donkeys

STOMPin' PaL

Back when he lived on Prince Edward Island, centennial walker-to-be Hank Gallant played some kitchen parties with an older fellow from down the road in Skinners Pond by the name of Tom Connors, who only later got the nick-name "Stompin'" Connors. The great troubadour of this land was first introduced as "Stompin' Tom" at the King George Tavern in Peterborough, Ontario, on Dominion Day in 1967. He got the nickname for stomping his boot on a piece of plywood to keep time to his songs as he tried to be heard over boisterous crowds.

shod, as no blacksmith had shoes small enough to fit them. Every night, she rubbed salve into their hooves. She immediately abandoned the notion of riding, determining that she would walk the entire way, too.

DeKelver's centennial trek was planned as a homage to the Overlanders, a group of about 115 settlers, all men but for one woman and her three children, who travelled from Ontario to the British Columbia Interior in 1862. After arriving in Fort Garry (present-day Winnipeg), the Overlanders hauled Red River carts to Fort Edmonton, where they traded the carts for pack horses. A returning party of gold miners from the Cariboo fields encouraged them to follow the Yellowhead Pass through the mountains. Indian guides were hired to lead them through the treacherous passage.

The group broke up into smaller parties. They suffered great privation along the way, coming close to starvation. One group became stranded by floodwaters, only to be rescued in the nick of time by a trailing party. Later, they lost many provisions and four died by drowning and of exposure after their canoes carved from hollowed-out logs capsized in rapids on the Fraser River.

A smaller, trailing group, which included the woman and her three children, tried to get to the goldfields by following an overland route, purchasing one hundred head of cattle and horses. Too late, they discovered that they would need to travel along the Thompson River. The horses were loosed and the cattle slaughtered. The group built canoes, but lost two men in an area of rapids known as Hell's Gate. At long last, the group arrived in Kamloops on October 12, 1862. The next day, Catherine O'Hare Schubert, who had made the journey while pregnant, gave birth to a baby girl, whom she named Rose—a sister for five-year-old son Gus, three-year-old Mary Jane and a one-year-old infant. Her husband, Augustus, a carpenter, went off to work in the goldfields.

The story of the Overlanders was well known in the North Thompson region of British Columbia. DeKelver wished to honour brave Catherine Schubert and to promote the Yellowhead Route while celebrating Canada's Centennial. An overland trek of her own seemed the most fitting way to do so.

The DeKelvers moved to the Clearwater Valley in 1959—before telephone service had even reached the district—and settled on an eighty-acre farm alongside Candle Creek. Three years later, they purchased one hundred ewes and rams, as well as a grazing lease on nearby Trophy Mountain. They tripled the size of the herd. It took three days to move the herd from farm to meadows, giving Ida a sense of what confronted her as she planned her journey. Both worked as guides in the area, even getting a chance to name some of its features, such as Buck Hill, which Ida named for the plentiful deer in the area.

Later, a forty-metre waterfall along Third Canyon Creek would be named Ida Falls in her honour. Before Ida embarked on her journey, she and Emil spread out a road map to plot likely stops along the Yellowhead Highway, along which she planned to travel. She wrote letters to local clubs and dignitaries announcing her project and seeking assistance. A typical response came from Dr. E.M. Martinuk, a chiropractor who headed a Centennial Committee in Saskatchewan. He wrote: "I would like to offer you a free stay (for yourself and the donkeys) as you come through Humboldt. I do hope your trip will be uneventful and may God keep you safe in your journey."

The letter is included on a Facebook page called "Yellowhead Museum."

Having plotted her path, Ida next took her camera to film natural scenes in Clearwater, including her own ranch and the unspoiled wilderness of nearby Wells Gray Provincial Park. She put together a film promoting the area, covering the cost of processing by charging local businesses ten dollars to have their advertisements inserted in the movie. The Chamber of Commerce in Clearwater decided to sponsor her trip as a means of promoting motor travel along the Yellowhead Highway, which was still in the process of being improved and paved.

On her first day, Ida walked twenty-six kilometres east to Vavenby, a mill town, which she reached in the afternoon. She showed her film at the Legion Hall before spending the night with a local couple.

She tramped forty-five kilometres on her second day, stopping at the Trimble farm at Avola, where once again she showed her film.

A lean, wiry figure, hardened by labour on her ranch, Ida wore loose dungarees and a pair of boys' size 5 shoes with soft leather uppers and a sole so thick that she would feel stubble underfoot only in the final two days of her walk. She held her hair in place with a kerchief, the wind whipping her bangs. Work gloves protected her hands from the wind and from chafing as she held onto the rope on which the donkeys were leashed. The monotony of walking through wilderness accompanied only by two beasts of burden did not bother Ida, for whom solitude was familiar from working in isolation life on the ranch. Besides, she liked how the pace made her feel. "It makes your muscles and nerves really alive," she said. "Your lungs are better for the breathing that goes with steady walking." On the third day, Ida was put up at the Tote Road Inn, which offered "cottages, souvenirs, confectionary" in Gosnell, a tiny wayfarers' stop, named after the province's first provincial librarian and archivist, at the confluence of the North Thompson and Albreda rivers. During World War II, an internment camp for Japanese Canadians was established in the hamlet. Work crews from the camp repaired and improved the unpaved highway. In

Ida DeKelver's centennial project involved retracing the steps of the Overlanders, pioneers who travelled over the Rocky Mountains to the goldfields in the British Columbia Interior. Ida and her donkeys, named Bill and Jack, walked from British Columbia to her birthplace province of Saskatchewan. *Photo: Saskatchewan Teachers' Federation*

a daily diary published after her trek, Ida recounted a "very warm welcome" from the innkeepers. Two days later, she arrived in Valemount, to hear gathered schoolchildren cry, "The donkeys are coming!"

As word of her trip spread, she was greeted along the highway by well-wishers who brought her coffee, doughnuts, sandwiches and, on one memorable occasion, roast chicken from a café up the road. "I proved the old Canadian hospitality is as much alive as it was a hundred years ago," she said.

On her fifth day on the road, she walked as far as she'd anticipated, so camped out in a field, spreading out her bedroll between the donkeys. They were placed as sentries, to alert her to any intrusions by wildlife. The following night she slept at the picnic grounds at Lucerne, a railway ghost town on Yellowhead Lake, thirty-seven kilometres from Jasper.

Ida crossed the provincial border at about one o'clock on September 23. She was met at the Jasper Park gates by park officials and Jasper chamber of commerce executives. They invited her to attend a musical show, while the donkeys were put up in government barns. Byron Moore, the railway station manager, and his wife offered to put Ida up for the night. (Moore, an air force veteran of World War II and a train buff, would be one of twenty-three passengers killed in the fiery Hinton train disaster in 1986, when the Via train in which he was travelling was struck by a freight train.)

At the eastern end of the park, Ida stayed at the Circle M, a dude ranch. Some miles further on, she arrived in Hinton, where the proud citizenry took her on a guided tour of the pulp mill. Her reward was a night in a motel. The following night she was once again kipping down in a field off the highway, between Bill and Jack. The younger donkey had fallen lame, so in Edson a cobbler was asked to fashion some footwear for the hobbling critter. Jack "is

MUSHING IT UP

Blake Brown, a twenty-three-year-old Edmonton house painter, was so thrilled by the adoption of the new maple leaf flag that he became driven to make a grand gesture to celebrate the Centennial. He decided he would go as far north as possible, to Tuktoyaktuk, north of the Arctic Circle, where he would mush a dog-sled team more than two thousand kilometres south to Edmonton in time to celebrate the Mukluk Mardi Gras, a popular winter carnival.

Brown moved to Inuvik, where he was taught to drive a sled and to care for dogs, to survive in the wilderness and to read a topographical map. He failed to convince a partner to join him, or to find companies willing to sponsor him.

Reckless, driven, foolish, he set off on his own: one inexperienced man with two sleds and two teams of dogs, heading south on the frozen Mackenzie River in the dead of winter. He fell into drifts taller than a man, often had to lead the dog teams himself, and suffered from the merciless cold.

After forty days, he reached a reckoning. "I'd been sleeping in −70 weather," he told *National Post* journalist Roy MacGregor in 1999. "My hands were frostbit. My feet were frostbit. I remember saying, 'Brown, you're not so tough.' I turned around and headed back to Fort Good Hope and took the first plane out." The *Winnipeg Free Press* ran a brief story on page 60, with the headline: "Musher Gives Up—Decides to Fly."

Brown later became a firefighter and then fire chief in Delta, a suburb of Vancouver, where snow is rare.

likely the only donkey in Canada that can boast of owning a pair of boots," the *Edson Leader* proclaimed.

The weather turned and outside Evansburg, Ida was "cold [and] miserable day and night."

On she walked, reaching Edmonton on October 3, continuing on to Vegreville, an agricultural town with a large Ukrainian population. (Later, in 1973, a giant *pysanka*—Ukrainian Easter egg—was built to mark the centennial of the Royal Canadian Mounted Police.)

Days passed. Ida kept walking, through Vermilion (named for the red clay in the river valley) and Kitscoty and the border-straddling city of Lloydminster, where the donkeys were "the main attraction and were treated very well by everyone," according to her diary as published by a local newspaper.

As her trek continued through her home province, the odd figure of this determined woman, accompanied by donkeys, became something of a celebrity. Newspapers regularly reported on her progress as she made her way through Maidstone and Delmas and into North Battleford, where Barry Conkin, the local Centennial Committee chairman, hailed her as "the Number 1 ambassador for the Yellowhead Route."

She was met on the outskirts of Saskatoon by a city official and a hotel manager. A photographer captured the tired-looking woman shaking hands with men in suits who looked out of place on the prairie scrub. After several radio and television interviews, the latter of which she later described as the most frightening event of her journey, Ida was put up in the Sheraton-Cavalier Motel, where the donkeys were allowed to graze on the grass before staying overnight. A huge crowd greeted her in Humboldt, where they gathered to see her films. She had become a folk heroine in the district. The three hundred students at St. Peter's College in Muenster invited her to join them for lunch, while she was also invited to a wedding at St. Gregor.

At long last, on October 25, a cold day during which she faced a steady blast of eastern winds, Ida arrived on the outskirts of Waneda. She was followed into town by a parade of cars, including some carrying her relatives from the Paul family of Kuroki, a nearby hamlet. She had completed an unaccompanied overland trek of fourteen hundred kilometres—marking along the way, in quiet solitude, her forty-fifth birthday and a wedding anniversary—a journey made in homage to a century-old act and in tribute to a country marking its hundredth birthday.

Two months later, she returned home to British Columbia, this time travelling by train. A special edition of the *North Thompson Times* newspaper carried a banner headline on the front page: "WELCOME HOME IDA DEKELVER and Congratulations on Your Achievement from the TIMES and all the People of Clearwater." The issue included congratulatory advertising from Small's Shell service station, the Clearwater Esso service station, Braaten's Electric, the Big Horn Cafe ("Welcome home Ida, Jack and Bill") and a personal note from Rene of Rene's Beauty Bar: "My thoughts were with you all the way."

In 1975, Ida opened the Yellowhead Museum on her own property, to show off the more than three thousand historical artefacts that she had collected over the years. She became the district's unofficial historian. Her grand walk certainly had raised the profile of the Yellowhead, which was formally incorporated into the Trans-Canada Highway system in 1986—connecting Winnipeg to Haida Gwaii off British Columbia's untamed northern coast, and passing through Wadena and Clearwater along the way.

"Don't let anything interfere with good things you plan," she once said. "Don't let fear ever stop you. Think positive and don't look back. If you want to do something, or be something, start trying."

DRIVING: MODEL (T) CITIZEN STAN GUIGNARD

In the summer of 1966, a war veteran with a flair for publicity announced a plan to girdle the globe at the wheel of a 1915 Model T Ford.

Stan Guignard's transcontinental journey was designed to promote the Centennial. He gained the support of the Canadian Centennial Commission, which agreed to back the venture with three thousand dollars. The Commission also provided boxes of buttons, postcards and tiny Canadian flags, which he was to distribute on the journey.

"I spent six years fighting for Canada," said Stan. "Why not spend one year advertising it?"

The car, known as a "brass monkey" for its brass radiator, needed to be started with a crank. It had been bedecked in flags and centennial crests, and "Canada 1867–1967" was splashed in paint on its side. On the roof perched a birchbark canoe made by the Ojibway First Nation.

Dragging behind the Model T was a trailer filled with clothes, equipment and camping gear for the driver; his wife, the former Gladys Meredith; and their daughter, thirteen-year-old June, who was pulled out of school for a year's education on the road. The trailer was topped by a globe and a fluttering centennial flag.

This would not be Guignard's first attempt to cover vast distances in a jalopy.

After his overseas service in England and Europe with the Royal Canadian Engineers, he had returned to Ontario with his bride, whom he had married in London in 1943. The war left him with an insatiable case of wanderlust. In 1946, he convinced the chamber of commerce in Sudbury, Ontario, to back a transcontinental journey in a car cobbled together from the parts of a 1914 and a 1920 Model A Ford. He carried a canoe on the roof, promoting the city's upcoming winter carnival. Guignard (pronounced Gwee-*nard*) wore a plaid shirt and a tam-o'-shanter. In an era of clean-shaven men, his long unkempt beard garnered attention whenever he parked the car. He told reporters for newspapers along his 3,500-mile route that he was growing his facial hair in order to compete in the winter fair's "whiskerino" contest.

Back home, he bought what was thought to be a worthless chunk of land near Fourth Chute village on the banks of the Bonnechere River near Eganville in Renfrew County. A long roasting fork and a pistol thought to be of 1830 vintage had been found on the land, as had coins and other knick-knacks, all of which Guignard was convinced were evidence of an unrecorded confrontation between settlers and First Nations residents.

More importantly, the land included access to a largely unexplored warren of limestone chambers and subterranean passageways, accessible through a natural entrance reached after a tough scrabble over brush and fallen rock. As a new owner, Guignard had managed to explore only about three thousand feet into the branching caves, retreating for fear of losing his way.

Guignard envisioned the caves as a major tourist attraction, complete with a hotel overlooking the river, all modelled on the Mammoth Caves of Kentucky. "Hopes Eerie Bonnechere Caves May Become Tourist Mecca," declared a headline in the *Ottawa Journal*, a hint of skepticism clear in the wording. Guignard sold his interest in the site to partner Tom Woodward in 1955. For a time, Guignard acted as a guide while wearing a caveman's loincloth. (The caves remain a tourist attraction to this day, though closed in winter when rising underground water makes much of it impassible, allowing the bats to occupy the site unmolested.) The money from the sale was used to purchase a 1920 Model T Ford, the chassis painted a garish yellow, the fender and top red. For laughs, he painted the inscription "Atomic Plant" on the engine hood and an admonishment on the trunk: "Don't laugh. We all get old." A canoe on the roof carried a sign announcing "World's Tour."

Early in 1956, the bearded Guignard and Len Harding, a fellow veteran from Ontario, drove from Renfrew south to Miami on the first leg of what was intended as a two-year trip around the world, conducted at the hair-raising speed of 20 m.p.h. The car was capable of reaching double that pace, "but it wouldn't last five miles at that speed, so we keep it down to twenty," he said. Problems included replacing two valves on the side of the road; getting a

CROSS-COUNTRY by THUMB

Twenty-year-old Kurt Johnson, a gold-mine surveyor from the Northern Ontario mining town of Timmins, decided he wanted to see his country. He convinced the mayor and the police chief to write letters of introduction urging officials to help him on his way. The town's Centennial Committee commissioned an artist to create an oversized scroll on which was written: "Greetings to Canada and her capitals from Timmins, Ontario." The town mailed the scroll "c/o City Hall, Vancouver," where he was to launch his odyssey. They also agreed to offer some modest financial assistance to help him on his way—seventy-five dollars. A cheque was also mailed to the West Coast. Johnson talked a local firm into printing a thousand business cards reading, "Thank You for helping me in my Centennial Trans-Canada Hitch-hike Project."

On June 20, he got to the side of the highway, put out his thumb and waited. And waited. And waited some more. Cars and trucks whizzed by as the hot morning passed. Finally, a burly trucker stopped and picked him up. "Get rid of the silly circus outfit, kid, and dress like a normal person," he said.

In an article he wrote for the *Ottawa Citizen* in 2007, Johnson described dressing in "a top hat, claw-hammer jacket with twin tails, wide bowtie and boot spats—period costume, 1867." The odd clothes were soon shoved into his army duffel bag, and later sold at a loss.

After many adventures, Johnson got the scroll signed by the mayors or acting mayors of Vancouver, Victoria, Edmonton, Regina, Winnipeg, Toronto, Ottawa (where he also got the prime minister's signature), Montreal, Quebec City, Edmundston, Fredericton, Charlottetown, Halifax and St. John's. Mission accomplished. Almost.

Johnson later wrote that a reporter suggested he also obtain the signature of Newfoundland Premier Joey Smallwood, the only living Father of Confederation—which he did.

After returning home, Johnson handed over the scroll to the mayor as the final act of his 7,281-kilometre journey. Soon afterward, he got hired as a cub reporter at the *Timmins Daily Press*. Johnson wrote about his adventures for the *Ottawa Citizen*, where he was letters editor, a decade before. By then, he had been presented with the framed scroll, which had been on display in a local museum.

parking ticket in Washington, DC, where they also suffered a fender bender; and experiencing eighteen flat tires on the first leg of their journey.

They had planned to follow the Miami leg with a tour of the Gulf of Mexico before returning north through Houston, Chicago and Detroit. The second leg was to include sailing to England for a driving tour of Europe and Africa, including an excursion to Cape Town, South Africa, to be followed by sailing to Panama, driving through South America and sailing to Australia and New Zealand, with the final days of the world tour including drives into Russia and China, a hop to Japan and a final sailing to San Francisco. In the end, the men ran short of money long before concluding the exodus, which Guignard later revived as a centennial project.

At the time he announced his 1967 odyssey, he was driving a cab, having lost his job as a car salesman for General Motors shortly after he announced he was going to travel the world in a Ford. He'd also worked in construction and had been an amateur heavyweight boxer. For a time, the 220-pound man fought as a professional wrestler who grappled under the name "Northern Bear" and often had with him as a mascot a black bear cub named Joe.

The jalopy, which led the Dominion Day parade in North Bay in 1966, was to do the same in Centennial Year before heading for Montreal and the Maritimes with a planned trip to Britain via cargo ship. Guignard tried but failed to get a gas company and an airline to sponsor the trip. In the end, the family travelled as far as Montreal and decided, like so many others, to see the world on two man-made islands in the middle of the St. Lawrence River.

After their centennial misadventure, Stan and Gladys Guignard became managers of the Dionne Quints Homestead Museum, which at the time was next to the Pinewood Park Motor Inn along bustling Highway 11 near North Bay, Ontario. They greeted more than twenty thousand annual visitors to the log cabin, whose porch displayed five baby buggies once used to transport Annette, Emelie, Cecile, Yvonne and Marie. The quintuplets, born to poor French-Canadian farmers Oliva and Elzire Dionne on May 28, 1934, were a Depression-era sensation. They were to spend nine years on display in a tourist attraction.

Nine months after Gladys's death from cancer, Guignard set out on his final global challenge in a Model A. He completed the journey more than a year later, after driving 38,600 kilometres (and sailing another 40,200 km), enduring flat tires, a blown head gasket and a sputtering engine after he mistakenly filled up with diesel instead of gasoline—not to mention an earthquake in Japan and Typhoon Helen in Hong Kong. While in the British colony, he attended a gathering of antique car enthusiasts, where he met a woman named Hazel

Wytch. She returned to her home in Perth, Australia, where the motorist showed up soon after and they got married. "The Lord takes one," he told the *Toronto Star*, "the Lord gives one."

Guignard returned home fifteen months after having sputtered down the road. He was greeted as a hero in his hometown with a parade of antique cars, a civic reception on Main Street, and a fundraising dance. He had raised $300,000 for cancer research.

Projects at Sea

THE GREAT CENTENNIAL BATHTUB RACE

As Centennial Year approached, the mayor of Nanaimo, BC, called on Frank Ney to head a committee exploring a suitable anniversary celebration for the port city on Vancouver Island. Ney was the city's best-known salesman, a flamboyant character who owned with family members a successful real estate and insurance business.

One of Ney's realtors had an idea. George Galloway, whose own family's business ventures included operating a ferry, suggested that the city could show off its excellent harbour by promoting a race of water-borne bathtubs.

At first, Ney was skeptical. "I thought that was nonsense," he said. "But [George] was a good salesman and I didn't want to hurt his feelings." As a test, Galloway sealed a claw-footed tub to which he had added a rudder and several bleach bottles as floats. It was placed in a fish pond behind the realty office. It didn't sink. A further test awaited.

The tub was placed in the water on New Year's Day, 1967, during the annual Polar Bear Swim. It floated and, though slow, managed to putter along. Ney was sold. He began to throw his considerable promotional skills into organizing the Great Nanaimo-to-Vancouver Canadian Centennial International Bathtub Race, which was to be a tongue-in-cheek affair.

The race would not have been so memorable had it not been fronted by so congenial a character as Ney. Born in London, England, he was raised in Winnipeg, where his father acted as superintendent of several insurance firms. When the family returned to England in 1936, young Frank headed north to play hockey in Scotland, later skating for teams in Poland where he found himself when war broke out. He returned to England to enlist in the Royal Air Force, serving in Coastal Command before returning to Winnipeg aboard a hospital train after suffering ulcers. He drank a glass of buttermilk every night before bed ever after.

Ney's good-natured personality and tireless promotional skills made him the face of a race dubbed "good, clean fun" for "lavatory admirals."

The race date was set for July 30. A course was drawn from Departure Bay in Nanaimo to Fisherman's Cove in West Vancouver, a thirty-two-mile crossing of the Strait of Georgia, a usually placid inner sea but one not immune to choppy waves.

The rules were simple:

1. The tub should be a tub.
2. No outboard motors more powerful than six horsepower.
3. Each pilot had to wear a life jacket and be able to swim at least two hundred yards.
4. Each tub was to be accompanied by an escort craft.

Six weeks before race day, more than a hundred entries had been received, including submissions from beer waiters and business executives. Two weeks later, the number of contestants was up to 130. Entrants continued signing up until hours before the launch.

"We have bathtub enthusiasts from all over Canada entered and the tubs are still rolling into town," Ney said, days before the event. "There were bathtubs all over the harbour the other night, practicing."

Among the entrants were tubs representing the CBC; first-year medical students at McGill University in Montreal; a group calling itself the International Establishment of Adventurers, Gentlemen Bathers and Cricket Players; and the self-proclaimed Burnaby Drinking Team. (The name "seemed to convey exactly what we were trying to accomplish," said president Jim Winton.) Each entrant received a scroll and the Royal Order of the Golden Plug, an ordinary bathtub plug and chain painted gold.

The wacky flotilla included all manner of plumbing vessels, from heavy, cast-iron claw-footed tubs anchored by two-by-fours to sleek, lightweight tubs made from glass fibre. One tub had hydrofoils on the side, while an entrant from Campbell River on Vancouver Island constructed a "tubamaran" with tubs on either side of his power plant. Other craft were powered by sails or oars, while one tub had a cycling-pedal arrangement by which the pilot powered a paddlewheel. "We are going to show the world," Ney pronounced in mock seriousness, "that Canada leads in bathtub technology."

An indigenous dancer named Leslie John performed a pre-race ritual expressing hope that all would race without injury.

Ney attended events dressed like a Mississippi River gambler in a cutaway coat, vest and gold watch on a chain. He carried a silver-tipped cane in one hand and a cigar in the other, while a straw boater sat on his head at a jaunty angle. All the ballyhoo attracted attention from CBC, CBS in the United States, BBC in Britain and a film crew from Denmark that had been on the island to shoot another event. Ney requested a naval presence, but a rear admiral at the Royal Canadian Navy's base in Esquimalt balked, saying a destroyer would not be able to manoeuvre around so many small craft. Instead, the RCMP boat *Sidney*, two Canadian Coast Guard cutters and more than two hundred escort vessels bobbed in the waters of Departure Bay alongside 208 tubs waiting for the start signal. After a delay and a false start, Ney managed to set off a flare and the race was on.

Thirty seconds later, the tub carrying George Dorman foundered and capsized, earning him the Silver Order of the Toilet Plunger (an ordinary bathroom tool painted silver). Another eighty contraptions failed to make much headway from the harbour, perhaps not surprisingly considering how "refreshed" some sailors were by the time of launch.

Many of the tubs were decorated in idiosyncratic fashion. Dr. Howard McDiarmid, a Social Credit member of the Legislative Assembly for Port Alberni on Vancouver Island, rode a tub painted white with a red cross on the port bow, a pennant carrying the word "Help" flying from the starboard side. The politician wore an all-white outfit covered in a clear, waterproof shell, making him look less like a doctor and more like an escapee.

The floating survivors of the oddball flotilla chugged, sailed and oared across the strait. Bob Robinson led the way, only to have his engine stall about five hundred yards from the beach in West Vancouver. He jumped overboard to tow his tub across the finish line. Meanwhile, Rusty Harrison of Richmond, BC, landed first, in a tub sponsored by the White Rock Travel Agency. He arrived three hours and sixteen minutes after Ney had fired the starting flare, earning a one-hundred-dollar prize and the Centennial Order of the Bath.

Only forty-six tubs made it across the strait. The lack of casualties, other than a few bruised egos, was a relief.

The finish line had been taken down and the race concluded when officials realized that one tub was still out on the water. A crew of ten from Gabriola Island, off Nanaimo, had left with all the other crafts, but had fallen further and further behind. Led by "admiral" Clyde Coats, a twenty-six-year-old contractor, the ten members took turns in the tub, while the others rested in a fishing boat skippered by Henry Silva. They were out on the strait as the wind rose and the sun set, slowly heading eastward through the night. One of the teenaged women on the crew fell overboard; another crew member had to go underwater to untangle the propeller of the fishing boat; and all were soaked by spray as gale-force winds whipped the strait. The team arrived at Burrard Inlet on the other side of the strait some thirty hours after setting out.

The Vancouver Island city of Nanaimo got in on the centennial fun by organizing a bathtub race across the Strait of Georgia to Vancouver. Dr. Howard McDiarmid, who represented a neighbouring provincial constituency for the governing Social Credit party, wore a hospital gown while aboard a makeshift craft named SS *Sacred*. He foundered in Nanaimo harbour. *Photo: Library and Archives Canada*

"Superb bathtub seamanship," crowed Ney, "and sheer courage."

The bathtub race was expected to be a one-off, but the interest generated in the zany contest led the organizers to form the non-profit Loyal Nanaimo Bathtub Society. A brewery became a sponsor and the race attracted competitors from around the world. Several future victors hailed from Australia, though locals remained competitive. The 1970 winner was George Dorman, who had been the first to sink in Centennial Year. Ney was named Admiral of the Fleet and changed his gambler's costume for that of a swashbuckling buccaneer. He was elected mayor of the city a few months after the bathtub race, a post he held for twenty years, while simultaneously serving for three years as the city's Member of the Legislative Assembly alongside Dr. McDiarmid. The mayor's Black Jack pirate persona became so associated with the race that a bronze statue of him in this attire was erected overlooking a harbour on whose silty bottom rest the remains of countless makeshift race shells, including that of George Galloway's original tub.

Projects in the Air

ONE-HUNDRED-DAY JOURNEY: THE CENTENNIAL HELICOPTER

A whirly-bird descends from the heavens, the wake from the propeller stirring up dirt and debris causing waiting dignitaries to turn away and protect their eyes. Once the dust settles and the blades of the Enstrom F-28 stop rotating, the welcoming committee can see into the cockpit. On the pilot's side sits Frank Ogden, who served as an air-force flight engineer in World War II. He has taken leave from his job as a therapist at a British Columbia hospital to indulge an ambitious centennial project: a one-hundred-day, ten-thousand-mile transcontinental journey by helicopter.

The white helicopter displays a hodgepodge of colourful symbols painted onto the fuselage, including the Canadian flag, the centennial logo, and the ten provincial crests. The legend "Canada: Centennial Panorama" runs from the cockpit nearly to the rear rotor.

In the co-pilot's seat rests an oversized fuzzy doll known as an Ookpik, a snowy owl crafted by the Inuit artist Jeannie Snowball. Ogden disembarks from the machine with his arms laden with gifts: hand-painted enamel plates, centennial coin presentation sets, novelty cans of fresh British Columbia air, tins of bowhead whale meat and blubber known as *muktuk*, and smaller Ookpik dolls made by Snowball and other co-operative members in the northern Quebec village of Fort Chimo (now Kuujjuaq).

After a polite exchange, Ogden would take selected dignitaries for a spin in the helicopter. More than five hundred would buzz their town or city, including politicians, centenarians, beauty queens, television cameramen and other worthies.

"We take part in centennial celebrations wherever we go," the pilot told the *Toronto Star*. "I think I've taken about forty mayors up in the past eleven days, but it's really something special for the youngsters."

One of the lucky civilian passengers was David Lockey, a nineteen-year-old youth born with cerebral palsy. His mother, Rita Lockey, campaigned for her son to get a decent education at a time when disabled people were regarded as a nuisance in the public-school system. The school he attended in the Toronto suburb of Scarborough wasn't able to provide him with the kind of assistance he needed, including aid in using a public bathroom. Two months after a newspaper story appeared describing his mother's efforts to find the young man a home in which to live, he was invited as a guest aboard the Centennial

Helicopter. He was given a buzzing tour of the Toronto waterfront and a spectacular aerial view of downtown skyscrapers as the sun set.

Ogden had picked up the Enstrom helicopter soon after it rolled off the assembly line in Menominee, Michigan. Governor George Romney was on hand for the event. Ogden told workers and officials at the luncheon that followed that he had spent five years examining helicopters from the Soviet Union, Czechoslovakia and other countries before settling on this American machine. "We are going to carry a lot of people with important necks, so we had to consider the safest helicopter," he told the gathering. Of course Ogden brought gifts, including a miniature carved totem pole for the mayor, Ookpiks for the reporters and tins of whale meat.

His first chore as pilot was to circle the airport before returning to hand a package of letters to the local assistant postmaster. The grand transnational tour was to begin after he flew the 'copter to St. John's, Newfoundland, before meandering westward. His itinerary included Expo 67 in Montreal and the Pan American Games in Winnipeg, as well as such aeronautic celebrations as the Abbotsford Air Show in the Fraser Valley and Skyway '67 in Brandon, Manitoba, which also included a race between four giant helium-filled balloons, as well as a performance by the Golden Centennaires, the precision flying team that was a precursor to the Snowbirds.

His cargo included sacks of letters that would receive special Centennial Helicopter postmarks. Joining Ogden was Chuck Diven, a magazine photo-journalist whose role it was to chronicle the journey in images. Philatelists from around the world sent envelopes known as commemorative covers to Ogden in care of P.O. Box 1967, New Westminster, BC. They hoped to have these envelopes franked with a special Centennial Helicopter postmark. Stamp designs for the project included depictions of a helicopter-to-hovercraft transfer, a kayak-to-helicopter delivery, and a stagecoach-to-helicopter pickup at 100 Mile House in the dusty British Columbia Interior.

The helicopter was trailed by a Citroen limousine outfitted with ham radio-broadcasting equipment that was capable of reaching operators around the world. The ground-support vehicle included a replica of the time capsule in which Ogden was to preserve newspaper clippings about his journey. He also gathered the signature of all passengers who rode in the craft.

Ogden felt capable of repairing his airship without the aid of a mechanic. "I carried a screwdriver, a pair of pliers (to avoid burning my fingers when checking the oil dipstick), a can of spray wax to clean the fuselage and a bottle of cleaner for the windshield," he said. "That, plus a couple of rags, my oil can and grease gun, is it. I found I needed nothing else."

Helicopter pilot Frank Ogden (centre) presents gifts to two officials from the Pacific National Exhibition in Vancouver. Ogden flew the Centennial Helicopter across Canada in 1967. He later became a futurist who billed himself as Dr. Tomorrow. *Photo: City of Vancouver Archives*

In October, he wrote a letter to the manufacturer that a local newspaper ran:

> *This is my 77th day of steady flying in the machine. No "down time" to date. Nice to be aboard such a dependable machine. During the last five days I have flown well over 1,000 miles over the most desolate sections of Northern Ontario. Most of the time solid bush without a landing spot of any kind. It was most reassuring to be in the Enstrom. I've never felt so safe in a helicopter. The same feeling carried me over the provinces of Nova Scotia, New Brunswick, Quebec and Ontario.*

The air journey ended on Vancouver Island. The province of British Columbia was suffering a bit from centennial fatigue by the time the helicopter arrived. Premier W.A.C. Bennett employed hoopla to maintain the popularity of his Social Credit party, so the province had earlier marked centenaries in 1958 of the founding of British Columbia as a Crown colony and in 1966 of the union of the colonies of British Columbia and Vancouver Island. A fourth centenary, to commemorate the province's joining Confederation, would be observed four years later, in 1971.

A plastic time capsule including copies of newspapers from across the land, as well as books, posters and photographs of a nation celebrating a landmark birthday, was sealed in a small park across the street from the lawn of the provincial Legislature. A bronze plaque reads: "The British Columbia time capsule contains records of the centennial years 1966 and 1967. Placed in Confederation Garden, New Year's Eve 1967. To be opened January 1, 2067."

Many of those whose centennial projects gained them attention from Canadian newspapers returned to their previous anonymity after 1967. Not Frank Ogden. Born in Toronto to English parents who planned to immigrate to the United States, he'd been hustling since he was a boy selling peat moss and breeding rodents in a Philadelphia suburb. He worked as a busboy and as a deck hand on a Cuba-bound banana boat before enlisting in the Royal Canadian Air Force in 1940. He flew patrols over the North Atlantic from a base in Newfoundland. After the war, Ogden enrolled in medical studies at the University of Manitoba, soon dropping out to work as a salesman of a product called the Minute Mop.

Daring in both temperament and deed, he established a flying record that stands unrivalled to this day. In 1953, he lifted off from Toronto Island Airport at the controls of a Mooney M-18 Wee Scotsman, soaring to an unprecedented level of 19,400 feet, an altitude that no light plane had ever achieved in Canada. "The record has never been broken," Ogden told the author Chuck Davis decades later. "Mainly, I suspect, because most pilots are sensible enough to want twenty to thirty gallons of gas left in the tanks to get back. I flew up until I ran out of gas and glided back to the same airport."

An adventurer with wanderlust, Ogden went to British Columbia after he read a magazine article about a hospital in New Westminster that offered a unique therapy to cure psychiatric ills.

He showed up unannounced and asked for a job. His qualifications? As he told Jake MacDonald of *The Walrus* in 2007:

I told them I was well qualified to work as a guide into "inner

*space" because I'd flown flying boats and survived helicopter
crashes, and set a dangerous high-altitude record in a single-
engine Mooney. I told them adventure was my game.*

Hollywood Hospital, a private clinic in an old mansion set among holly trees, took him on as an unpaid worker. In time, as he told MacDonald, he came to be the chief therapist, administering doses of LSD to Hollywood celebrities and Vancouver society matrons alike.

He interrupted his time at the private hospital to complete his centennial tour. The next year, he launched a think tank on Grouse Mountain overlooking Vancouver, to which he invited those who believed that imagination could solve the world's troubles. After a short stint as an instructor at the Ontario College of Art (where he listed his job description as "provocateur"), Ogden presented himself as a curriculum innovator, teaching "psychic renovation" at the New England College of Art before joining the Dreyfuss Division of the Future at Fairleigh Dickinson University in New Jersey.

When not in the classroom, he piloted sloops, freighters and a mini-submarine in the Caribbean. After undergoing a fire purification ritual in Haiti, Ogden invited a voodoo priest to present a series of lectures, complete with rattles and rum bottles, on a campus in Madison, New Jersey.

In 1989, the members of the exclusive Explorers Club in New York named him a Fellow, joining such adventurers as mountaineer Sir Edmund Hillary and astronaut John Glenn. By then, Ogden was ensconced on a houseboat next to yachts moored in Vancouver's Coal Harbour, his floating home. It was stocked with computers and video recorders fed by satellite dishes that brought to his watery den broadcasts from around the globe. Billing himself as "Dr. Tomorrow," he earned a healthy income as a futurist, offering businesses a guide to upcoming technologies and infuriating professors—among others—with his predictions of their coming demise. He told the *Los Angeles Times* that more than a hundred professors at the University of Alberta had walked out of his presentation when he insisted that teaching was obsolete in the new age of learning. "If you can flip a switch for electricity and turn a tap for water, why can't you just press a button for knowledge?" he asked rhetorically. "I think the day is coming when you can have any information you need delivered electronically, either to home or school." Two years later, the World Wide Web went live. In time, it would provide access to Ogden's own life story, including his transcontinental helicopter jaunt in celebration of the Centennial—just as he had predicted.

A GOBSMACKER: *HELICOPTER CANADA*

Eugene Boyko spent eighteen months dangling from a helicopter while shooting spectacular images of the land below. Once, he got so excited about a shot over the Detroit River that he leaned out only to remember that he had neglected to tether himself to the 'copter. He managed to hang on—for which his audiences can be grateful.

The resulting fifty-minute film, titled *Helicopter Canada*, a National Film Board documentary, offered audiences a bird's-eye view of Canada as it had never been seen before. Boyko rigged weights and counterweights to counter the vibrations from the whirlybird. The result included images that gobsmacked audiences—a lone prospector in an unending expanse, the Golden Boy atop the Manitoba Legislature, a football game seen from just behind the quarterback as he accepts the snap. A daredevil shot of the lip of Rainbow Falls before dropping over the edge must have left audiences breathless. Boyko even got a shot of the Beatles leaving Toronto airport in a limousine, Paul giving a "thumbs-up" from the middle seat while John waves from the back.

"I wanted to do this for Canada," Boyko said at the time. "We have such a beautiful country, but how many people can fly around and enjoy it? So I felt we could do that, and I felt that this was the time of the century to make it."

Boyko, known as "Jeep," logged twenty-four thousand kilometres in the air in order to capture forty thousand metres of film. All of it was shot from an Alouette II turbine helicopter, at elevations ranging from six thousand metres to just above sea level for shots of the schooner *Bluenose II*.

The film was sponsored by the Centennial Commission as a travelogue for audiences abroad, especially in the United States, while also offering Canadians an unfamiliar look at their own land. A document of its time, the film is accompanied by narration by Stanley Jackson from an arch script by Donald Brittain and Derek May.

Contemporary reviews were complimentary. Marshall Delaney described it in *Saturday Night* magazine as "a triumph of mature documentary art." Joan Fox informed *Globe and Mail* readers that "if this film doesn't stir your Canadian blood, nothing will." One odd criticism came from an RCMP officer who feared that the images of the nickel smelter in Sudbury would aid the Soviets in planning an attack on Canada.

Helicopter Canada was nominated for an Oscar for best documentary feature, but lost to the British production *The War Game*, which depicted a devastated Britain following a nuclear attack.

The film was released by the National Film Board with English and French narration, and was subsequently translated into another dozen languages for global distribution. It was shown in Canada along with feature films. The movie made its television premiere the following June, and more recently was added to the roster of documentaries available for streaming online by Netflix Canada and the Documentary Channel in the United States. Domini Clark of *The Globe* thought the movie did not age well, finding that it "provokes more cringing than pride." Still, Boyko's handiwork captured marvellous images from above the giant Manicouagan dam in Quebec, and the curved towers of Toronto City Hall that generate awe even in an age of drones with Go-Pros.

PILOT HEADS FOR POLE

John Cameron made a pass over the ice floe. He circled and made another pass. Then, a third. Followed by a fourth and a fifth. On the sixth attempt, he bounced his single-engine de Havilland Otter onto the floe. Later, he would call the landing "almost routine." He had not quite reached his flight's destination, the North Pole.

"There was a lot of open water around," he said, "so we landed a mile away and just drifted over the Pole."

Once there, Cameron planted a centennial flag. He was accompanied by four scientists: Leif Lundgaard of Norway, Bob Lillestrand of Minneapolis, and Hans Weber and Axel Geiger from the Dominion Observatory in Ottawa. The scientists were gathering information about the polar continental shelf. The expedition made seismic, gravitational and celestial observations, including

SKYDIVING EXTRAVAGANZA

William Hardman, a twenty-three-year-old sky-diver, completed one hundred parachute jumps in one day, a centennial project that happened to be a world record. After completing his first jump, Hardman had to wait at the airstrip in Abbotsford, British Columbia, as a thick fog enveloped the Fraser Valley. Once it lifted three hours later, he was again back in the air with pilot Herb Porter.

"When I landed in the target area, I would walk or run to a pickup vehicle and then ride back to the airstrip about three hundred yards away, where the plane was waiting," Hardman said at the time. He jumped on an average of once every eight minutes, taking a fifteen-minute break after the fiftieth jump and the eighty-first, which surpassed a mark set earlier by two American skydivers. About ten thousand people were on hand to applaud as he made his hundredth jump at 9:30 p.m., seventeen hours after his first.

of the satellites streaking above, while also examining the ice and water. An electrical transformer was plunged into the frigid waters, to sink to the ocean floor some 13,800 feet below.

Cameron's landing on May 14, 1967, was believed to be the first completed by a single-engine aircraft at the Pole.

Navigation was not easy under the conditions of constant Arctic daylight. To take star shots using a special theodolite necessitated waiting until a fog bank rolled in.

Even the takeoff was risky. Cameron had landed on a floe about a thousand feet long, which gave him just enough icy, bumpy runway for takeoff.

A Myriad Of Projects

CRAFTING CENTENNIAL QUILTS

Eldra Robertson, a seamstress of note in the village of Chase in British Columbia's wild Shuswap Country, spent six months manipulating appliqué and embroidery for her entry in the province's quilt competition. She chose as her inspiration a series of historic images from the province's gold rush days.

Her quilt included panels showing sternwheelers plying the Fraser River, camels used to carry supplies to the goldfields, and Royal Engineers marking the Cariboo wagon road. One of her panels showed the Overlanders rafting into Kamloops in 1862, the event that inspired Ida DeKelver's centennial walk through the Rockies.

Eldra Robertson was born in Vancouver and moved to Mound Ranch near Chase as a youth. (She was five years old when her mother died from influenza in 1918.) She developed a reputation as a cook and a decorator, and was known for her design of floats in the village's May Day parades.

Her centennial quilt won first prize, worth five hundred dollars, when exhibited at the Pacific National Exhibition in Vancouver in 1967, after which the Provincial Museum in Victoria acquired the piece. It was loaned to the Quesnel Museum in 1976 and was formally transferred to its collection in 2013. It is on display at the museum today.

Countless centennial quilts can be found in local museums and as family keepsakes across the land. A grocer in Saint John, New Brunswick, spent three months creating a quilt featuring the centennial symbol. It was displayed in the city's centennial office.

Beatrice Ziegler of Alberta spent two hundred and fifty hours on her quilt, which included flowers, provincial crests, and symbols of industry. It also bore

Eldra Robertson (left) and Irene Summers pose with the prize-winning centennial quilt.
Photo: Quesnel & District Museum and Archives

the names and addresses of ladies' auxiliary members of the Canadian Legion. The quilt earned a special class award when entered into the women's category at the Medicine Hat Exhibition and Stampede.

To the guild members, known for their artistic vision and nimble skill in creating family keepsakes, the Centennial offered a chance to craft a legacy for the nation.

THIS, THAT AND THE NEXT THING

Micro-Canvases: How sweet it was. Margaret English, a Winnipeg homemaker known for her cake-decorating talents, used tiny decorator tips to reproduce the provincial flowers of all provinces and territories on the surface of a cube of sugar, surely one of the tiniest canvases ever faced by an artist. The Manitoba crocus was created with mauve petals and a yellow centre surrounded by tiny green leaves. English, married to a medical technician, presented small boxes of thirty-six decorated cubes as gifts to her friends and family, some of whom undoubtedly plopped the tiny artworks into their tea.

A detail of Eldra Robertson's centennial quilt depicts the paddlewheeler *The Beaver* in the harbour off Fort Victoria, a scene recreated in cloth from John Murray Gibson's painting *Steel of Empire. Photo: Quesnel & District Museum and Archives*

Replica: Gerry Bordeleau of Ottawa turned the family dining-room table into a showplace for his replica of the Parliament Buildings, including a metre-tall Peace Tower topped by a Canadian flag. The replica, which took six weeks to build, was covered with almost twelve pounds of candy-covered chocolate and nineteen pounds of icing sugar.

Salvage: Toronto's skin-diving Kennedy family, including eleven-year-old Gavin, spent much of the year at the bottom of the St. Lawrence River, where they salvaged bottles, capstans, lanterns and rudders from sunken vessels.

Steam Engine: Awolt Franz Loose, a sixty-eight-year-old retired car mechanic in Lethbridge, Alberta, decided to construct a working scale model of a steam engine like those he had seen working the prairies as a boy. He'd come to Canada from Germany with his parents in 1905, finding work as a blacksmith's assistant. "I used to help sharpen up the ploughs and then take them out to the farmers, many of whom used steam engines similar to the one I've built," he said. Gasoline-powered tractors replaced steam engines in the 1920s, and Loose became a car mechanic. He built his intricate steam engine, a mass of tubes and valves capable of hauling a half-ton, without drawings of any kind. "I knew what a steam engine looked like," he explained to the *Lethbridge Herald*, "and I just used my imagination."

Preservation: In Milton, Ontario, the Halton County museum got a total of $31,857 from three levels of government to collect and preserve sleighs, buggies, stage coaches and horse-drawn agricultural implements.

No Sex: Sigmund de Janos, a civil engineer, film producer and aspiring screenwriter, wrote a comedy script titled "How to Ban That *!+/! Bomb," dedicating it to the prime minister for his efforts to foster world peace. The script, for which he had Peter Sellers and Elke Sommer in mind as stars, borrowed the theme of Aristophanes' play *Lysistrata,* in which women of a city deny their husbands sex until war ends.

Beards: More than five hundred men in Smiths Falls, Ontario, entered a beard-growing contest, seeking to emulate the hirsute appearance of the Fathers of Confederation.

Costumes: Employees at the head office of Manitoba Hydro turned the clock back a hundred years by wearing period costumes.

Derby: The town of Gatineau, Quebec, organized a soap-box derby for boys.

Restoration: Douglas Evans, a businessman, restored and moved into a log cabin dating back to 1861 that was situated near a major intersection northwest of downtown. In the Toronto suburb of Oakville, a couple spent $6,000 to restore their pre-Confederation home.

Art: Winnipeg businessman John Crabb took as his centennial project the gathering of works by late Western Canadian landscape artist Walter J. Phillips.

The collection was then prepared for display at any schools or museums interested in studying the works.

Letters: Jane Bennett, a reporter for the *Woodstock Sentinel-Review* in Ontario, made it her mission to write personal letters to fellow citizens living in isolated hamlets in the north. "I am telling them the history of this city and our present activities and asking in return to have details of their way of life," she said. "In this way I hope to forge a permanent link between my correspondents and Woodstock." In her first month, she got a reply from the principal of the school in Resolute Bay. Her plan was to have all the correspondence bound for presentation to the local library.

Lake-comber: Victoria Smaizys, a sixty-year-old Winnipeg homemaker and immigrant from Lithuania, decided to become a prairie beachcomber, searching the shoreline of Manitoba's lakes for stones, driftwood and broken glass smoothed by water for use as ornaments, sculptures, and, needless to say, paperweights. "Collecting is like an illness," she told the *Winnipeg Free Press.* "It can't be cured." She saw in some rocks and refuse famous visages such as those of Alfred Hitchcock and Charles de Gaulle. Not surprisingly, her home had a surfeit of flat surfaces for her to display her treasures.

Vibra-Art: At St. John's-Ravenscourt private school in Winnipeg, the Sixth Form students (Grade 12) decided to mark the Centennial by replacing three large, glass-block windows in the gymnasium with three artistic panels carved from Vibrafoam, more commonly used for sound insulation. The dominant image in each window was fire (symbolizing the mind), a tree (the body) and an eagle (the spirit).

Anti-Stereotype: In Winnipeg, the First Nations students at Assiniboia High organized a conference for all Winnipeg students called "Meet the Indian." The ambitious centennial project was designed to challenge stereotypes and to end enmities based on cultural background.

Library: Students at Laurentian High in Ottawa donated a two-thousand-volume library to the Golden Lake Reserve (today, the Algonquins of Pikwàkanagàn). About one thousand dollars from school fundraising projects was left for the purchase of additional books and supplies.

Pit Dwellings: The Soowahlie Band of Sto:lō people in British Columbia's Fraser Valley worked to restore ancient pit dwellings on reserve land, some thought to have been occupied as recently as 1860.

Blood: Molly Saunders of Ottawa launched a drive to find 1,967 blood donors for the Red Cross Society.

Student: The congregation of St. Paul's Anglican church of Dauphin, Manitoba, received a bequest from the estate of late businessman Edward Mayo, some of which they used to cover the costs of study in Uganda for theological student Eliphaz Maari, a twenty-seven-year-old schoolteacher. The congregation agreed to pay for her education over three years as a church centennial project.

Clothing: Charity began closer to home for Audrey Wright of Ottawa, who gathered clothes to be delivered to poverty-stricken families in Brantville, New Brunswick.

Patriotism: For all the public works, all the construction and the flash of Expo 67, it was the spirit of ordinary Canadians that best expressed the joy of living in the peaceable kingdom. "Public response was the most refreshing part of the whole Centennial," John Fisher told the *Toronto Star*. "It suddenly became popular to show our patriotism. People had more fun than I thought they would."

TRANSATLANTIC PROMOTION: YOUTH TREK

Ken Swaisland had a vision of being a youth diplomat for Canada, spreading the word about a wondrous nation celebrating its one hundredth birthday. Born in England, he had thought Canada a land of log cabins in a pristine wilderness until he arrived in Toronto. His ambition in 1967 was to dispel myths about Canada while touring Europe.

The twenty-four-year-old advertising copywriter convinced the Ford company to let him borrow a truck for five months. He then got a camper on loan from a manufacturer, about three thousand dollars' worth of cameras and film from Kodak, and three cartons of centennial bumph (including pins and leaflets) from the government.

Joining him on the trek were Ray Smith, a twenty-five-year-old reporter with the *Toronto Telegram,* and artists Jennifer Cline, twenty-one, and Heather Cooper, twenty-two.

As organizer, Swaisland, an earnest fellow of serious demeanour, insisted that the group did not plan to go on the bum on their travels.

"We're tired of the stories of young people like us living on LSD in Yorkville," he said at the time, referring to a Toronto neighbourhood of cafés popular with youth. "We've done well in Canada and we want to repay some of this, as well as gain a wealth of experience."

Swaisland's sales acumen nearly failed him when it came to arranging passage to Europe. "We had a hard time finding someone to pay the ocean freight charges for the trailer-truck," he told the *Toronto Star*. "I phoned thirty-seven shipping companies who turned us down, but, finally, the Russian government came across and said they'd take it free on their ship."

The quartet travelled to Europe aboard the Baltic Shipping Company's *Aleksandr Pushkin*, a Soviet freighter that carried passengers. The truck was parked on the main deck for the transoceanic voyage. "Canada Youth Trek" and a red maple leaf were painted on the driver and passenger doors.

They toured Britain, Scandinavia, East and West Germany, the Benelux countries, Italy, Spain and Yugoslavia, all the while speaking to classrooms and public meetings about Canada. They took thousands of slides along the way. Venice was a highlight, as was touring London's Carnaby Street at the height of the Swinging London era. "It was fun," Cooper recalled of the tour, when contacted recently. "We got to see all the backstreets and all the places tourists who stay in hotels never get to see."

They even managed to cross the Iron Curtain. It took several hours to clear customs at Checkpoint Charlie, the crossing between East and West Berlin, a hot spot in the Cold War. On their return, they handed out maple-leaf pins to border guards and surreptitiously left behind Expo stickers on guard posts. By the end of their European sojourn, they had logged more than nineteen thousand kilometres.

They returned to Canada, once again aboard the *Pushkin*, in time for the final days of Expo.

Smith, the journalist, stayed behind in Europe. In a peripatetic career, he covered earthquakes and massacres, spending five years at the *National Enquirer*, where he was assigned to provoke Sean Penn and to blame the Three Mile Island nuclear meltdown on Jane Fonda, one of the supermarket tabloid's favourite targets. He later reported for the *Edmonton Sun* and its sister paper, the *Toronto Sun*. Smith contracted hepatitis C when inoculated for cholera with a dirty needle while covering the Mexico City earthquake in 1985. He died in 1994, aged fifty-two.

Jennifer Cline (left), Ray Smith and Heather Cooper examine a road map, while Ken Swaisland waits in the cab of a truck on loan. The four young Canadians spent the summer of 1967 travelling around Europe, including behind the Iron Curtain, to spread the word about Canada and centennial celebrations. *Photo: Boris Spremo* / Toronto Star

Swaisland went on to own an art gallery in Vancouver before founding a company promoting the use of sustainable products. He died in 2013.

Cline worked as an illustrator and graphic designer for a Toronto advertising agency before taking up painting, her favourite subject being her own leafy Toronto neighbourhood known as The Beaches. She was a well-known figure in the area, easily spotted on her bicycle forays because of her red hair. She died in 2016.

Not long after her transatlantic adventure, Cooper joined with Robert Burns in a ground-breaking design firm. Among their clients: two young Americans with an idea for a Canadian-identified shoe (and later clothing) company. Cooper came up with a beaver atop branches for Roots, soon among the most successful logos in Canadian history—and now better known and with greater global circulation than the centennial symbol that she shared with Europeans fifty years ago. After taking up painting, she was commissioned to paint a portrait of Pope John Paul II during his Ontario tour in 1984. She now lives in a home studio in the forest north of Baltimore, Ontario, where a youthful caper and the spirit of the age that inspired it are fondly remembered.

Canadian cuisine

The Canadian Home Economics Association gathered recipes from its 1,019 members to create a cookbook of Canadian cuisine as a centennial project. Sally Henry, editor of the Laura Secord Canadian Cook Book, said an all-Canadian menu could include tourtière from the Gaspé, fiddleheads from New Brunswick, a wild rice casserole from Saskatchewan served with Yukon sourdough bread and Ontario butternut spice cake. Henry said she believed such desserts as lemon bread and butter tarts likely developed as uniquely Canadian foods.

The humble butter tart was declared a staple of Canadian cuisine, one of many such observations made as a modest people took stock of their first century as a nation.
Photo: MSPhotographic / Thinkstock

Happy Birthday(s)

January 1, July 1 and Other Fresh Starts

IT WAS A year in which young and old were feted for sharing a birthday with the country. Babies born on New Year's Day and on Dominion Day were hailed as "centennial projects," while centenarians were asked for their reflections on a country with which they had aged. At least one baby hit a jackpot, though she would have to wait until 1988 to collect.

Centennial Babies

The birth notice from the Kathnelson family included a modest joke. It read: "Jerry and Karen (née Swenson) are most happy to announce the arrival of their Centennial project, a daughter."

The couple may have been the first to joke about their baby as a Centennial project, but they would not be the last. It became common to see such references sprinkled among the birth notices in Centennial Year.

The arrival of a New Year's baby is almost always a joyful event (even if it means a tax deduction was missed by a matter of minutes). In 1967, people celebrated two groups of centennial babies: those born on January 1 and those arriving on July 1.

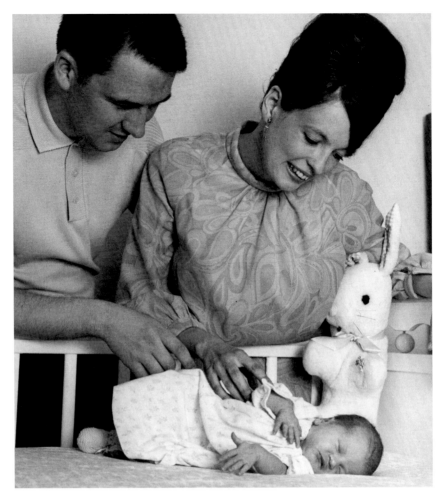

Allan and Elizabeth (née West) Burdett dote on baby Andria Louise Burdett, who was born in Winnipeg at 12:33 a.m. on Dominion Day. The family was chauffeured home from the hospital in a limousine, and a housekeeper was sent to cook and clean for the baby's first week at home. *Photo: University of Manitoba Archives & Special Collections*

Newfoundland Premier Joey Smallwood claimed on behalf of his province the first Canadian centennial baby when a daughter was born to Mr. and Mrs. Eldridge Thorne of St. John's at 12:06 a.m. The premier made his claim based on the province's half-hour time-zone advantage over the Maritime provinces.

Ottawa General Hospital claimed the year's first birth with an eight-pound, eight-ounce boy born at the stroke of midnight. The Ottawa Civic Hospital disputed the claim, insisting it had learned that the boy was born in the old year.

Metro Toronto's first baby was a six-pound, six-ounce girl, a sixth child born to thirty-two-year-old Jane Beal. The girl arrived one second past midnight at Toronto East General Hospital. Toronto's runner-up was David Neil Klein, who arrived three minutes past midnight at the new Mount Sinai Hospital.

In Windsor, Ontario, Laura and Ralph Shreve celebrated the birth of a daughter, whom they named Princess and who would grow up to be a registered nurse.

In Chilliwack, British Columbia, the first centennial baby, Glen William Bustin, did not arrive until the morning of January 3. His parents received gifts from area merchants.

A bigger fuss was made over the first babies born on Dominion Day. In Winnipeg, the arrival of Andria Louise Burdett at 12:33 a.m. on July 1 meant that mother and child would return home in style. A chauffeur-driven Cadillac was put at the family's disposal for a week, while a housekeeper was assigned to clean and cook for the baby's first week at home.

In Ottawa, a baby boy was born in Ottawa General to June and Gerald Sarazin as the Peace Tower bells tolled the century of Confederation. Later in the year, Judy LaMarsh personally presented young André with a Centennial Medallion. Fifteen other babies were born in Ottawa-area hospitals on Dominion Day. More than a thousand Centennial Medallions were mailed to other babies born on Dominion Day.

In Toronto, Carol Jane Tidd was born a minute after midnight, a delight for parents Frank and Edna, recent immigrants from England. The baby's photograph appeared in the newspaper, as it did again after her first birthday. At age seven, she got to meet the Queen; a photograph of the two could be seen hanging in the lobby of Scarborough Civic Centre.

To mark her birth, the suburban borough created a five-hundred-dollar trust fund, which she was to collect on her twenty-first birthday in far-off 1988. When that day arrived, she was presented a cheque for nearly two thousand

DEBUT FOR LITTLE PAMELA ANDERSON

The most famous of centennial babies—in retrospect, that is—was born in Ladysmith on Vancouver Island. Her arrival so excited her grandfather that he called the *Ladysmith-Chemainus Chronicle* to mistakenly report the birth of a grandson.

The seven-pound, three-quarter-ounce girl born at 4:08 a.m. on July 1 was named Pamela Denise Anderson. It would not be the last time that Pamela Anderson, star of TV shows such as *Home Improvement, Baywatch* and *VIP*, would be the subject of erroneous reports in the press.

dollars at Scarborough's Canada Day celebrations at Thomson Park. She planned to use the money to travel to Australia.

As for the Kathnelsons' centennial project, she grew up to be a scientist like her father and grandfather, and became an instructor at Lakeland College in Vermilion, Alberta. Her father, Jerry Kathnelson, is also known as the father of the programmable thermostat, which helps to reduce greenhouse gases.

Letting Loose on Dominion Day

By July 1, the initial reluctance to get fired up about the country's centennial had long since been replaced by a proud, excitable celebration. As Oscar Brand's song affirmed, Canada really had "Something to Sing About." Dominion Day was a chance to let loose.

"Ours is a good land," said Prime Minister Lester Pearson in a special Dominion Day statement.

Thirty thousand gathered on Parliament Hill, where they could gaze upon a marvel of a birthday cake—soaring six metres high, and decorated with the national coat of arms and provincial crests. After addressing Parliament, the Queen came out to cut the cake, using a knife that her father, King George VI, had used for a similar event in 1939. She cut into an insert of real cake at the forefront of the monstrosity. She could not know that the rest was fake, made of plywood and Styrofoam covered with 320 kilograms of icing sugar. The guests were served cupcakes.

Later, the Queen tossed a quarter into the fountain of the Centennial Flame—after cadging the coin from the prime minister. Prince Philip lived up to his reputation for pointed questions by asking a teenaged rock musician, "What kind of fertilizer do you use for your hair?"

Some fifty thousand Torontonians lined the downtown streets for a parade followed by a party in the square in front of the new, modernistic City Hall. Other parades were held in Toronto's neighbouring boroughs and suburbs. The festive feeling was not patriotic enough for some onlookers. "Canadians," complained celebrant Mary Kate Rowan, "are apologetic about being Canadian." More than twice the number of daytime revellers were on hand for evening celebrations, including some in period costume and men clean-shaven for the first time in months, after a barber who set up a chair in Nathan Phillips Square trimmed the also-rans in a beard-growing contest. There was square dancing, round dancing and go-go dancing, followed by fireworks.

CBC Radio rebroadcast Joseph Schull's "Century," narrated by Budd Knapp, a sweeping dramatic story about Canada's first hundred years that originally

Queen Elizabeth cuts a giant birthday cake on the steps of the Parliament Buildings in Ottawa. The cake was made of plywood covered by frosting save for a real cake inserted where the Queen was to make her ceremonial cut. She's using a knife her father used for a similar purpose on his 1939 visit. Guests to the Dominion Day celebrations on Parliament Hill were given cupcakes. *Photo: Library and Archives Canada*

aired, to acclaim, on New Year's Day. It was followed by a concert that was broadcast live from Place des Arts, featuring the Montreal Symphony Orchestra and the Mendelssohn Choir. The night ended with a professor talking about the legacy of Canada's first prime minister from John A. Macdonald's former home in Kingston, Ontario.

Billed as a "swinging" ninety-minute look at Canada, "The Spirit of '67" included music, archival photographs and comedy sketches, as well as birthday greetings from entertainment stars. Percy Saltzman was the host, with featured guests William Shatner, Don Harron and the Brassard Family. The variety special was followed by a more serious-minded program as author Hugh MacLennan looked at the forces of the 1860s leading to the creation of the nation.

"LAMENT FOR CONFEDERATION"

By 1967, Canadian audiences were familiar with Chief Dan George for his role as Ol' Antoine on *Cariboo Country*, the television show set in the British Columbia interior. He was a familiar figure when he took the stage for a Dominion Day celebration at Empire Stadium in Vancouver.

His impassioned address silenced the crowd.

"How long have I known you, Oh Canada? A hundred years? Yes, a hundred years. And many, many *seealnum* [lunar months] more. And today, when you celebrate your hundred years, Oh Canada, I am sad for all the Indian people throughout the land."

He told the audience how abundant forests provided food and clothing, how crystalline rivers flashed light in the sun, beckoning all to share in the aquatic abundance. The winds of the land reminded him how spirits once roamed the land.

The arrival of Europeans altered the relationship between man and nature. Foreign customs imported by the new arrivals served to alienate the indigenous people, whose defiance was met by an aggressive response.

"When I fought to protect my land and my home, I was called a savage," Dan George continued. "When I neither understood nor welcomed this way of life, I was called lazy. When I tried to rule my people, I was stripped of my authority."

His peroration offered a vision of a hopeful future in which people would not live in isolation, instead embarking on a better century than the previous one.

"Before I follow the great chiefs who have gone before us, Oh Canada, I shall see these things come to pass. I shall see our young braves and our chiefs sitting in the houses of law and government, ruling and being ruled by the knowledge and freedoms of our great land."

George Ryga's two-act play *The Ecstasy of Rita Joe*, about the tribulations of a young Aboriginal woman in the city, debuted at the Playhouse Theatre in Vancouver, heralding a new age for Canadian theatre. *Photo: Simon Fraser University Galleries*

Some partiers were older than the land they celebrated. Mary Larter sat on the porch of her Toronto home reflecting on her one hundred and six years. She had been born into a military family; her father had served as an officer under the Duke of Wellington at Waterloo.

The city of Weyburn, Saskatchewan, changed its name to Crocus to honour the fictional town found in the writings of native son W.O. ("Bill" to locals) Mitchell.

In London, England, the Queen Mother attended a service at Westminster Abbey commemorating the Canadian centenary.

A sombre note was struck in Canada's newest province, as Newfoundland mourned its war dead on July 1. The premier attended a graveside service for two Fathers of Confederation.

The *Toronto Star* published an editorial stating, "We Canadians are, right here and now, just about the luckiest people on this seething planet." Beside the editorial was a cartoon by the great Duncan Macpherson, portraying the prime minister waving the flag while leading a parade that includes the other political leaders. In the background, a man in a headdress plugs his ears.

That Dominion Day's most lasting message, to mark the beginning of Canada's second century, came not from the Queen or the prime minister but from a former longshoreman on the other side of the country. Born as Teswahno, he went by the name Dan Slahoot in English until sent to a residential school that forbade the use of native languages. He took his father's first name in English as his new family name. The world came to know him as Chief Dan George from his roles on stage (*The Ecstasy of Rita Joe*), on television (*Cariboo Country*), and in film (*Little Big Man*).

The sixty-six-year-old chief silenced a full house marking the Centennial at Empire Stadium in Vancouver with a searing soliloquy, "Lament for Confederation."

POPULAR LETTERS

The Companions of the Order of Canada are allowed to bear the letters "C.C" after their names. As it turned out, those letters also were used by the members of the Ontario Institute of Chartered Cartographers, undoubtedly a distinguished group in their own right.

The Order of Canada Is Born

The prime minister surprised the House of Commons with the announcement in 1967 of a major honour, to be known as the Order of Canada, created to recognize Canadians of outstanding achievement in distinctively Canadian fashion; those honoured would not receive traditional titles or hereditary privileges.

The rank of Companion of the Order of Canada was bestowed for "outstanding achievement and merit of the highest degree, especially in service to Canada or to humanity at large." Other honourees received a Medal of Services. The announcement of a uniquely Canadian honour system was the first since 1943, when the Canada Medal was created—though never awarded. The ranking would lead to controversy even before the Order had celebrated its first birthday.

Currently, there are three ranks: Companion, Officer and Member, the latter for "distinguished service in or to a particular community, group or field of activity."

Recipients of the Order of Canada were presented with a gold medal with white enamel, and a red maple leaf inside a red circle topped with a crown. It was to be worn on formal occasions on a ribbon around the neck. The six-leaf "snowflake" was designed by Bruce Beatty, an air-force graphic designer, who was inspired when walking to an officer's mess: "It started to snow just a little bit, just the odd snowflake coming. . . You can't be any more Canadian than that." Beatty would be made a Member of the Order in 1990.

The medals bear the Order's motto, *Desiderantes meliorem patriam*, Latin for "They desire a better country," from Hebrews 11:16.

(The release from the prime minister's office incorrectly cited Hebrews 12:16, which reads, "Lest there be any fornicators, or profane person, as Esau, who for one morsel of meat sold his birthright." Opposition Leader Diefenbaker harrumphed, "They can't even quote scripture correctly.")

In an editorial, the *Ottawa Journal* saluted the sentiment of the new honour, stating, "The idea of a titled aristocracy with fancy names is unnatural to North America" and declaring:

> *The old chess game of ten of everything in this ten-province country, of one of every race and religion, of treating all deputy ministers as equal, all retired generals as comparable—that will have to go. The distinction of distinctions must be that one distinguishes between the good and the excellent.*

The names of the first thirty-five Companions were announced on July 7. This elite group included opera singer Maureen Forrester, novelists Hugh MacLennan and Gabrielle Roy, poet F.R. Scott, painter Arthur Lismer, former prime minister Louis St. Laurent, first native-born governor general Vincent Massey and surgeon Wilder Penfield.

Among the Medal of Services award winners were hockey star Maurice "Rocket" Richard, Inuit artist Kenojuak Ashevak and Dr. Augustine Mac-Donald of Souris, Prince Edward Island, a general practitioner on the island for six decades, who once operated on the kitchen table of a farmhouse to re-attach the nearly severed feet of a farm boy.

When a second honours list, released in December, named Morley Callaghan as a Medal of Services recipient instead of as a higher-ranked Companion, the Toronto novelist rejected the medal. "If writers are being given Orders of the first class then I object to being one of the second class," he said.

A New Tory Leader–and Other Political Events

The Progressive Conservative leadership convention became the biggest political story of the year. Delegates chose Robert Stanfield, a lawyer and Nova Scotia premier, as a replacement for John Diefenbaker.

Stanfield went on to win a seat in the House of Commons in a November by-election. (That same day, the Conservatives retained an Alberta seat and

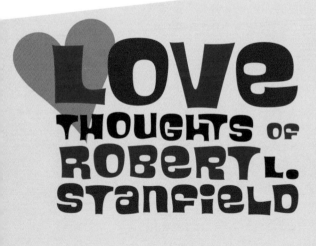

LOVE THOUGHTS OF ROBERT L. STANFIELD

Some who were planning centennial projects conceived do-good acts, a reflection of a less cynical age. Robert Lorne Stanfield, who at the time was Nova Scotia premier but would be national Progressive Conservative leader by year's end, told journalist Peter C. Newman that a worthwhile centennial project would be for "each Canadian [to] examine his own mind and surrender some prejudice against Canadians of another group." He personally promised to get Nova Scotians to love the people of Toronto for the duration of Canada's second century. The verdict is still out on the success of his pledge.

The four Maritime premiers gathered in the Confederation Chamber of the Provincial Building in Charlottetown, Prince Edward Island. On hand to mark the centenary of the Charlottetown Conference, one of three meetings leading to the creation of a new nation, were (from left) New Brunswick's Louis Robichaud, Nova Scotia's Robert Stanfield, PEI's Walter Russell Shaw and Newfoundland's Joey Smallwood. *Photo: Library and Archives Canada*

the Liberals did the same in Newfoundland.) He would end up serving as the federal PC leader until 1976.

When Canada's second century dawned in 1967, its people had elected a total of 2,608 fellow citizens to represent them in the House over the last hundred years. These included among their number Sir John A. Macdonald, the dipsomaniacal first prime minister; Amor de Cosmos, an eccentric newspaper publisher from British Columbia (who had been named William Smith at birth in Nova Scotia); and Louis Riel, the messianic Métis rebel leader, who was not allowed to take his seat as representative and whose life would end at the end of a noose.

The historical ranks also have included trailblazers (Agnes Macphail, the first woman to be elected to Parliament, and Douglas Jung, the first Chinese Canadian to be elected) and traitors (Fred Rose, a Communist exposed as a spy). Not surprisingly, more than one professional hockey player enjoyed the confidence of the people, some playing right wing (Howie Meeker, elected as a Progressive Conservative), others left wing (Red Kelly, elected as a Liberal).

As he lit the Centennial Flame to inaugurate a year of celebrations, Lester Pearson had served as prime minister for three years and eight months, all the while juggling a minority Parliament.

The year was only five days old when Rodger Mitchell, an Ontario pharmacist and Liberal member of Parliament, died in a Sudbury hospital. A by-election was held five months later, with the New Democrats winning the seat, while Liberal candidates prevailed in four other contests held simultaneously in Quebec.

Four provincial elections were held during Centennial Year, with incumbents winning re-election in all of them—the Social Credit party in Alberta in May, and Conservatives in Ontario and Liberals in Saskatchewan and New Brunswick, all in October.

Some political dynasties were soon to be toppled, as the conservative Union Nationale disappeared as a force in Quebec, while Social Credit eventually would collapse in Alberta and British Columbia, as well as on the federal scene.

The resignation of Robert Thompson as national leader of the Socreds in March 1967 gave a hint of the party's future travails.

In December, Liberal Prime Minister Lester Pearson announced his intention to retire from politics in the new year, wrapping up his career in the satisfied aftermath of centennial celebrations.

SCOUTS HONOUR CONFEDERATION GRAVES

The Boy Scouts of Canada marked the Centennial by laying wreaths on the graves of the Fathers of Confederation in ceremonies held across the country, from Nova Scotia to British Columbia.

In Victoria, Scouts attended Ross Bay Cemetery to honour John Hamilton Gray, a Prince Edward Islander who attended two of the three historic constitutional conferences (in Quebec, Charlottetown and London) that led the way to Confederation. Gray later served as a Supreme Court judge in the westernmost province.

On Dominion Day, similar services took place at Cataraqui Cemetery at Kingston, Ontario, the final resting place for Sir John A. Macdonald; and at

Côte-des-Neiges Cemetery in Montreal, at the graves of Sir George-Étienne Cartier and Thomas D'Arcy McGee. All thirty-six Fathers were honoured, a tribute that also had been performed on the occasion of the Diamond Jubilee of Confederation forty years earlier.

Over the years, some graves had fallen into disrepair. The federal government announced that it would underwrite the cost of maintaining the sites. "Canada has neglected a very sacred duty in not giving these truly outstanding Canadians the care their last resting places deserve," Northern Development Minister Arthur Laing stated.

The Girl Guides and Boy Scouts also gathered smooth river stones to be used in a cement rendition of the centennial symbol, a monument that would be placed in the grass next to Murney Tower in Macdonald Park on Kingston's waterfront.

HAND-WRITING THE BIBLE WITH POLITICIANS' INPUT

The congregation of Bethel Pentecostal Church required fourteen months to complete their centennial project, an entirely handwritten Bible. The Ottawa church enlisted participants from all ten provinces and from eighteen countries around the world. There were 1,189 contributors, one for each Bible chapter.

Prime Minister Lester Pearson selected as his verse Psalm 67: "God be merciful unto us and bless us; and cause His face to shine upon us." John Diefenbaker, the Progressive Conservative leader at the time, selected Psalm 121: "I will lift up mine eyes unto the hills from whence cometh my help." (Considering the difficulties Diefenbaker faced from colleagues on Parliament Hill, his selection had some perhaps unintentional irony.)

One of the first scribes to contribute, ninety-year-old Stella Maley, died before the project was completed. Another, an elderly woman from Shawville, Quebec, wrote: "I am in a wheelchair, my right leg amputated and my eyesight is poor. A friend of mine offered to write it for me. I said, 'No, that is my ask to do,' and I was glad to do it."

The completed "Centennial Handwritten Bible" was as large as an atlas, as thick as a dictionary, and weighed forty-eight pounds. It was displayed under glass in an oak cabinet specially constructed in the church's Sanctuary. The pages were turned at regular intervals.

5

Music and Festivals

Celebrating with Many a Song and Dance

MUSIC WAS IN the air all through Centennial Year. Gordon Lightfoot introduced an instant classic to a national television audience on the year's very first day. An official Centennial Anthem was commissioned. Politicians continued the age-old debate about a national anthem. And an energetic band leader dressed as a Pied Piper led children in a catchy pop tune instantly recognizable to anyone in 1967.

Official Music

"O CANADA" INCHES FORWARD

Canada began its one hundredth year without an official national anthem. The country moved closer to getting one in 1967, but ended its hundredth year short of the mark.

You'd think that a century would offer enough time for a nation to choose the music and lyrics of a song to honour a land and its people—even one as vast in territory and as diverse in population as Canada.

To be fair, politicians had come to an agreement about the music. It was the words over which they bickered. As they do to this day.

The Red Army Chorus thrilled crowds at Expo 67 with their massed voices. They also visited Ottawa, where they sang "O Canada" in the main entrance of the Parliament Buildings. *Photo: Library and Archives Canada*

In 1964, the federal government authorized a joint committee of Senators and members of Parliament to consider the official status of "God Save the Queen" and "O Canada." Two years later, the prime minister made a motion for the former to be recognized as the Royal Anthem and the latter as the national anthem. The committee continued to meet. By March 1967, they had reached agreement. The music for "O Canada" written by Calixa Lavallée in 1880 would be adopted with a notation added to the sheet music: "With dignity, not too slowly."

The committee also came to agreement regarding the French lyrics. The English words, however, remained contentious, as they have ever since Lavallée put music to a patriotic poem by Adolphe Routhier. His poem, commissioned by the lieutenant-governor of Quebec, opens with familiar words: "O Canada! Terre de nos aïeux,/ Ton front est ceint de fleurons glorieux." In 1906, T.B. Richardson took a stab at a direct translation, which won approval from Routhier. "O Canada! Our fathers' land of old,/ Thy brow is crowned with leaves of red and gold." Alas, the translation was denounced in Ontario for "reeking with Catholicism."

Two years later, Stanley Weir produced the version most familiar today, introducing "home and native land," "glowing hearts" and "true north, strong and free," not to mention a lot of "standing on guard"s (five of 'em). Even so, three revisions were made to his wording in short order.

A band leader and jingle writer, Bobby Gimby was inspired by seeing children at a St-Jean Baptiste parade to write "Canada," which became a second national anthem and the theme song for Centennial Year. *Photo: Ron Bull / Toronto Star*

In Centennial Year, the parliamentary special committee suggested replacing one "stand on guard" with "from far and wide," while also replacing a later "O Canada" with "God keep our land."

It was not until thirteen years after Centennial Year, in 1980, that "O Canada" would be proclaimed the national anthem with unanimous support from Parliament's two chambers, a decision rendered in time to mark the centenary of its first performance, if not the centenary of our fathers' land of old.

And in Popular Music...

Bobby Gimby's song "Canada" certainly got more airplay in the Centennial Year than the national anthem-to-be. In fact, the version featuring the Young Canada Singers was the top Canadian song in 1967, soaring to No. 1 on the RPM record chart.

The record, promoted by the Centennial Commission and familiar from television and radio play, did not hit stores until the third week of January. Dealers could not keep it in stock and the first shipment of 25,000 was instantly sold out. The national promotion manager for Quality Records predicted sales of a quarter-million, an unheard-of sum. One radio station vowed to keep it on the charts throughout Centennial Year. Several cover versions were recorded, including a Dixieland version by Jim McHarg and His Metro Stompers, an instrumental take by Ben McPeek with an orchestra, and a Mamas and Papas-style pop version by a band called the Department of Public Works. The impressionist Rich Little recorded a parody, lisping like Prime Minister Lester Pearson and harrumphing like Conservative leader John Diefenbaker.

Songwriter Gimby had been inspired by hearing Quebec children a few years earlier singing folk songs as they marched in a St-Jean Baptiste Day parade. In their boisterous innocence, he saw the possibilities of national unity through children's voice.

In April 1967, Secretary of State Judy LaMarsh presented Gimby with a gold record. (LaMarsh received a gold record of her own as a keepsake.) By May, sales had topped 200,000. "Canada" went on to be the best-selling Canadian record to that time, selling more than a half-million discs. More than 75,000 copies of the sheet music were sold. The song earned a special trophy at the Festival du Disque, the Quebec Grammys, as best English-language record. At year's end, Gimby was named a Companion of the Order of Canada.

Yet the sunny tune had a limited appeal beyond the year of its release, and decades later the record remains a staple at thrift shops and yard sales.

Even on July 1, 1967—Dominion Day in Centennial Year—not a single Canadian song was to be found on the nation's Top 40 charts and only "Canada" made the Top 100 on a chart based on store sales and radio plays. (The biggest song in all Canadian charts in 1967 was "The Letter" by the Box Tops, followed by "To Sir With Love" by Lulu and "All You Need is Love" by the Beatles. The poor performance by Canadian titles led to the introduction a few years later of Canadian-content rules.)

Gordon Lightfoot had set the bar high in 1967. One day into Canada's year-long birthday celebration, we already had a classic for the ages: "Canadian Railroad Trilogy," which Lightfoot had created for the CBC centennial television broadcast.

The three-part structure of "Canadian Railroad Trilogy" was influenced by Bob Gibson's "Civil War Trilogy," the song building up speed like a steam engine powering up. Lightfoot tells the story of men living on stew and bad whiskey as they conquered muskeg and mountain passes to link a vast land, not all of the labourers surviving the ordeal. The song would be released later in the year on his *The Way I Feel* album, "Trilogy" clocking in at six minutes and twenty-two seconds, an epic paean to the land and to the men who tried to conquer it.

Lightfoot played the ballad at the opening of the National Arts Centre in Ottawa two years later. Later still, he would meet the Queen at a Canada Day celebration. "She told me how much she loved the 'Canadian Railroad

Trilogy,'" he told the *Telegraph* newspaper of London in 2016. "She looked at me and said, 'Oh, that song,' and then said again, 'That song,' and that was all she said."

———

A NUMBER OF other songs have contended for popular status as the nation's unofficial anthem.

Oscar Brand, a folklorist born in Winnipeg but raised in Brooklyn, wrote a jaunty hymn to his native land, one of more than three hundred songs written by the longtime troubadour and broadcaster. Brand's "Something to Sing About" referred to all regions of Canada, a song of praise to a majestic country. Also known as "This Land of Ours," the tune became popular when covered by The Travellers. Brand hosted a television variety show with a folk emphasis in the mid-1960s. (One of his discoveries was an ethereal young woman from Saskatchewan named Joan Anderson, whom the world would soon know as Joni Mitchell.)

Movie actress Marlene Dietrich reinvented herself later in life as a cabaret singer. Her act at Expo 67 earned rave reviews. *Photo: Library and Archives Canada*

He once used the song's popularity to woo the woman who would become his wife, as he told CBC Radio's Michael Enright in an interview on Brand's ninetieth birthday. The couple was on their first trip together to Canada when he accosted a passerby on the street. "I walked over to the first person I saw, as unlikely a singer as you ever saw, and said, 'You ever hear of a song that goes, 'From the Vancouver Island?'" and before you knew it he was singing the song." If some stranger on the street knew Brand's song, then everyone Won the street must. He figured that she would have to be impressed. "If you've got the people of your country singing your songs," Brand said, "then you're a hero."

The Travellers also had a popular anthem in their Canadianized version of "This Land is Your Land," a reworking of Woody Guthrie's response to Irving Berlin's "America the Beautiful." The Canadian lyrics referenced Canadian landmarks instead of American ones.

Perhaps the strongest claimant as unofficial anthem was written in the bright aftermath of the centennial celebrations. Dolores Claman, a classically trained musician, was paid eight hundred dollars in 1968 to write "The Hockey Theme" for broadcasts of "Hockey Night in Canada." She'd never seen a game before, imagining two gladiators battling on ice as she wrote the music. It was orchestrated by Jerry Tosh. The pair worked together to create "A Place to Stand (Ontar-i-ar-i-ar-i-o)," with lyrics by her husband Richard Morris. The song was the theme for a movie of the same name that aired at the Ontario pavilion at Expo 67.

BOBBY "NIMBLE LIPS" GIMBY

The advertising agency Vickers and Benson won the advertising and promotions contract for Centennial Year. The Toronto outfit rented space next door to the Centennial Commission, in the felicitously named All-Canada Building at 1000 Yonge Street. One day, agency president Bill Bremner got a call from an old acquaintance named Bobby Gimby, a diminutive, bespectacled bandleader with an ebullient personality. They had met years earlier when Bremner handled advertising for Eaton's. Gimby had written a song for centennial, pronounced it "pretty good," and thought the boys at the agency might like to hear it.

The owlish musician was one of Canada's most successful creators of pop songs and jingles. Robert Stead Gimby was born in the town of Cabri, Saskatchewan. He spent the early part of the war years as lead trumpeter with the touring orchestra of Mart Kenney and his Western Gentlemen. He left to join the troupe known as The Happy Gang, who lent their name to a popular weekday variety program on CBC Radio, where they played patriotic tunes during the war (including a daily rendition of "There'll Always Be an England"). Along the way, he gained the nickname "Nimble Lips" for his horn playing.

Gimby (pronounced jim-*bee*) later fronted his own band, playing night clubs in Toronto and resorts in nearby Muskoka, not to mention high society gigs. He'd written "The Cricket Song" with comedian Johnny Wayne and the

"Canada" RIGHTS

The Centennial Commission held the rights to "Canada" during 1967, after which they reverted to Bobby Gimby as the song's creator. In 1971, he donated all future royalties from the song to the Boy Scouts of Canada.

THE YEAR CANADIANS LOST THEIR MINDS AND FOUND THEIR COUNTRY

Jazz legend Thelonious Monk performs outdoors at Expo 67. His concert was recorded live and is now available on CD. Other jazz greats to perform at Expo include Roy Eldridge, the Dave Brubeck Quartet, and George Wein and the Newport All-Stars. *Photo: Library and Archives Canada*

novelty song had been recorded by Ray Bolger, who had played the Scarecrow in *The Wizard of Oz*. Other tunes of his were sung by the likes of Peggy Lee and Max Bygraves.

In 1962, he was in Asia working for a tobacco company when he entered a government-sponsored competition to write a song to mark the pending federation of Malaysia. He dashed off an anthem after breakfast one morning and sent it in. Although, as a foreigner, he was ineligible to win the $300 contest, his "Malaysia Forever" was declared an unofficial anthem by the federation's prime minister. Gimby hired local musicians and found a girls' convent choir to handle the vocals. A beguiling, if somewhat saccharine anthem, the song topped the country's charts.

All of this influenced what he had in mind for his own country's centennial.

Bremner invited him to his office. Gimby showed up wearing a cape and carrying a long staff topped by a crown. He began to sing for a small audience.

"We heard 'CAN-AH-DA one little, two little, three Canadians' for the first time," partner Terry O'Malley recalled years later in an online posting. "It was instantly infectious. We went across to the Centennial office and played it for them. Eventually, the entire agency was ready to follow Gimby anywhere."

The problem was that no one had planned on having a last-minute addition to the centennial line-up.

"The government brass in Ottawa had already settled on a Centennial Hymn and an anthem," agency vice-president Al Scott told the *Canadian Magazine*. "But I knew neither would work." Scott said:

Canadians tend to be complacent patriots. And the sophisticated city slickers in the newspaper business have almost made it a sin to express enthusiasm about our nation. What we needed was a grabber. A stirring flag-waver that would make everyone feel, "Gee, this is a real good opportunity."

Rare Recordings

Edward Balthasar Moogk, a radio host, convinced the Centennial Commission that his own hobby was a worthwhile national project. A lifelong record collector, he suggested that Canada needed an archive to preserve the early sound recordings of works written, sung and produced by Canadians. The commission agreed and gave Moogk funds to acquire rare recordings.

With his long career in radio and the recording industry, no one knew the history better than Moogk. He began at station CKCR in Kitchener, Ontario, where he used the professional on-air name of "Ed Manning," and later served as host of the national CBC Radio program *Roll Back the Years*. The show's name became the title of a history that he published in 1975.

Moogk was the first head of the Recorded Sound Collection, from 1972 until his retirement in 1979—by which time the holdings included thirty-three thousand recordings.

The pioneer discographer's own collection of four thousand recordings formed the nucleus of the collection now at Library and Archives Canada.

Children in colourful ethnic costumes sing at a folk art festival in Toronto held as part of centennial celebrations. *Photo: Library and Archives Canada*

The agency convinced the Centennial Commission to give its imprimatur to the Gimby song, which was released on Quality Records early in 1967. With lyrics in English, French and then English (and, on the flip side, in French, English and then French), the stars of the recording were billed as the Young Canada Singers. In fact, they were eight ten-year-olds from Toronto, known as the Craddock Kids, under the guidance of Laurie Bower, and another eight ten-year-olds from Montreal who were directed by Raymond Berthiaume.

Officially titled "Canada"—though, given the extended syllables in the singing, often spelled "Ca-Na-Da" —the appealing tune soon became inescapable. It could be heard playing on the radio, on the Confederation Train, and at Expo 67, where it easily overshadowed the fair's official theme song of "Un jour, un jour"/"Hey Friend, Say Friend."

Gimby rode the Confederation Train across the land, leading children at each stop, a centennial Pied Piper spreading unabashed patriotism and joy. He wore a two-tone green cape and a scarlet scarf around his neck, while blowing into a long, gold-painted heraldic trumpet festooned with beads and century-old coppers glued to papier-mâché.

MUSICAL POTPOURRI

The Sugar Shoppe: This vocal quartet from Toronto hit the middle of the Canadian charts in 1967, topping out at No. 40, with a cover of Bobby Gimby's "Canada." The flip side was "Thoroughly Modern Millie." A sunny, upbeat arrangement by pianist and singer Peter Mann gave the two-man (Mann and Victor Garber), two-woman (Lee Harris and Laurie Hood) group a Mamas-and-Papas sound. They recorded soon after forming and only made their first public appearances owing to the success of the single. Known for their harmonies and bubblegum pop, they charted a handful of songs in coming years, including a cover of Laura Nyro's "Save the Country." Garber went on to a stellar acting career, first on stage and later in television and Hollywood, including a role in the blockbuster movie *Titanic*.

LP Project: RCA Victor released an anthology of Canadian musicians in a series of seventeen long-playing records, the most ambitious project ever undertaken by a label. Each jacket displayed a masterpiece by a Canadian artist from the collection of the National Gallery, while every album included an eight-page booklet describing the titles in the series. The works of thirty-two Canadian composers were included in the series, with performances from soloists and such groups as the Montreal Baroque Trio and the Vancouver Chamber Orchestra. The albums were presented as gifts to guests who stumped the panellists on CBC Television's current events quiz show, *Front Page Challenge*.

Cashing in: Artists in every genre sought to cash in on interest in the Centennial. Billy Van's *Centennial Polka* was a fundraiser for the Indian-Eskimo Association of Canada, supported by the Steinberg's grocery-store chain, which

GUITAR·a·THON

In Edmonton, ten guitarists played their instruments nonstop for one hundred hours, as a six-stringed salute to the Centennial. Taking a five-minute break every two hours, they surpassed the previous world record of fifty-eight hours and nine minutes set in 1966 by strummers in Illinois.

was marking its fiftieth anniversary. The flip side had the French recording "Fêtons Fêtons Fêtons" by Jacques Michel. *Gospelaires with your Centennial Album* featured a gospel quintet from Fredericton, New Brunswick. From the same province, Ned Landry of Saint John released *Canadian Old-Time Fiddle Centennial Tour*. The music group the Brothers-in-Law, featuring four police officers (hence the group's name), issued *Exposé 67*, a collection of critical songs in satirical fashion, a style that the group described as "folk-knock."

Meri-juana Brass: In 2009, Ottawa newspaper columnist Earl McRae bought a second-hand album for $1.99 at a thrift store. *Downbeat 67* featured the Merivale High Concert Band—and its cheeky offshoot, the Meri-juana Brass—playing a set of high-school band standards. The band had joined other schools in a performance at Expo 67. The LP had been recorded during practices in the school cafeteria and was sold only to friends and family, an exclusive souvenir of a special year.

Canadian Discount: The Record Club of Canada, which offered a 30 percent discount to members who paid a $5 subscription fee, marked the Centennial by offering a further reduction on Canadian titles. These were indicated in the club's publication by a centennial symbol in the margin next to the images of the album covers. (For the kids reading: a record club mailed vinyl records to your home in the days before digital downloads.) The front cover promoted four Canadian releases: a two-LP set of Seiji Ozawa conducting the Toronto Symphony; *Canadian Centennial Celebration* by the Black Watch of Canada's Regimental Pipes and Drums; Gordon Lightfoot's *The Way I Feel*; and Rich Little's comedic *My Fellow Canadians*.

Centennial Hymn and Anthem

As a writing assignment, a hymn presents certain difficulties. First of all, it is directed at a deity. That's a tough audience.

A Centennial Hymn, to be sung on so august an occasion in a nation of many peoples and two official languages, had to be composed with great care. Canada was described at birth as a Dominion, the word taken straight from the Christian Bible. Yet the hymn had to be acceptable to the Canadian Interfaith Conference, a group established by the Centennial Commission to coordinate religious activities during the celebratory year. At the time, the Conference represented twenty-eight religious faiths—a number that, by 1967, had grown to thirty-four—and the hymn had to satisfy all without offending any.

More than fifty hymns were submitted. The one chosen was written by Reverend Kenneth Moyer, minster of Lundy's Lane United Church in Niagara Falls, Ontario. (The church was built atop old British battlefield lines in the War of 1812. Casualties of the battle had been buried there.) Reverend Moyer composed three stanzas of eight lines each.

One line in the opening stanza echoed a similar line in "O Canada," while other parts of the hymn paid homage to the Lord's Prayer. The hymn had its share of "Thy"s and "Thou"s, not to mention "hast"s and "Heaven"s. A French version (not a direct translation) was written by Ronald Després, an Acadian poet, musician, author and playwright who spent years on Parliament Hill as a translator of House of Commons debates. The music was composed by Rex Lelacheur, a musician born in the Channel Islands at Guernsey, who founded and directed a fifty-voice mixed choir in Ottawa called the Rex Lelacheur Singers.

The hymn was first sung in public at the composer's studio. Lelacheur sang the melody in a rich baritone, as Reverend Moyer joined in, for an audience of reporters.

The Canadian Interfaith Conference had commissioned the hymn early in 1966. The Conference chairman was Lavy Becker, representing the Canadian Jewish Congress, who headed a nineteen-member secretariat. The group agreed to produce a booklet of hymns and prayers suitable for all the religious faiths represented by the Conference, which was to be distributed at the Christian pavilion at Expo 67. They were behind schedule. "I am frightened by the amount of work that still needs to be done," Becker said.

Becker was born in Montreal to Russian immigrants. As a youth, he had been among the founders of an Orthodox synagogue. After earning a degree at McGill University, he was ordained at the Jewish Theological Seminary in New York. At war's end, he was sent to Germany, where he worked with refugees in displaced persons camps under the auspices of the Joint Distribution Committee. Back in Montreal, he founded Congregation Beth-El, Montreal's first Conservative synagogue to have mixed seating. In 1960, he founded Dorshei Emet, the Reconstructionist movement's first congregation in Canada. (The movement regards Judaism as being in constant evolution and responsive to modernity.) "He was the incarnation of Jewish concern and devotion, a broad and encompassing view of Jewish life, and a deep, unquenchable love of learning," Rabbi Gunther Plaut of Toronto once said.

By the time he was named to the Conference's board of directors, Becker had left the rabbinate and had been working in his family's equipment-man-ufacturing business, while also contributing to many humanitarian causes.

A striking tableau set by two dancers with the National Ballet of Jamaica, one of many national dance troupes to perform at Expo 67. *Photo: Library and Archives Canada*

His great skills managed to bring disparate groups to agree upon the contents of a bilingual booklet of prayers, as well as upon the hymn, copies of which were sent to nineteen thousand clergymen, in every church, synagogue and mosque across the land.

Less than two weeks after the hymn was unveiled in December 1966, another work—also commissioned by the Interfaith Conference—was introduced. The English version was known as the "Anthem for the Centennial of Confederation."

It was to make its debut on Parliament Hill at the end of the month, to usher in the Centennial Year. (In a practice session for the unveiling, a closed-circuit television link allowed Dominion carillonneur Robert Donnell in his Peace Tower studio to observe Nicholas Goldschmidt conducting the National Capital Area Centennial Choir on the lawn.)

The music for the *Hymne à l'occasion du centenaire de la Confédération canadienne*—as the anthem was known in French—was composed by Healey Willan, who drafted a choral arrangement to be sung by nine or more voices. Born in 1880 in Balham, now part of Greater London, England, Willan immigrated to Toronto in 1913 to head the theory department at the Toronto Conservatory of Music (later the Royal Conservatory of Music). He served as organist and choirmaster for several churches, as well as for choral and operatic societies, while also handling duties as music director at Hart House at the University of Toronto. He was regarded at the time as Canada's most notable composer.

The lyrics for the anthem were written by Robert Choquette, a poet, novelist and radio playwright who had been appointed deputy commissioner of the National Centennial Administration in 1963. Four years later, he was living in Bordeaux, France, as Canada's consul general. (Like Willan, he was not a native Canadian, having been born in New Hampshire.) Lyrics for the English version of the anthem were adapted by John Glassco, the Montreal-born poet who lived in the Eastern Townships village of Foster.

Willan, born just thirteen years after Confederation, died six weeks after Centennial Year concluded.

Both the hymn and the anthem were quickly forgotten after the celebrations ended. That was an appropriate fate for the forgettable hymn, according to Peter Ackroyd, the public relations director for the Centennial Commission, who had a better opinion of Choquette's work on the anthem. As Ackroyd wrote in his 1992 memoir, *The Anniversary Compulsion*: "The Prince of Poets did a magnificent job: soaring and sensitive, the words deserved to live and could be revived with pride any year, any century."

Louis Riel Opera

The baritone Bernard Turgeon sang some of opera's most coveted roles. He made his debut with the Canadian Opera Association (now Canadian Opera Company) at age twenty-three; four years later, he played the peasant Masetto in *Don Giovanni*. By then, he'd won a national CBC competition as the nation's top vocalist. Leading roles followed. He portrayed Junius in *The Rape of Lucretia* at Stratford, Ontario, and played Bartolo in *The Barber of Seville* for Sadler's Wells Opera in London, England. He was the first Canadian ever to be hired by the famed company (now known as the English National Opera) as a principal singer.

Turgeon performed with American opera companies, the warmth of his voice and the depth of emotion that it conveyed attracting a considerable following. For all his growing reputation outside his native land, Turgeon returned home and to his roots to find the role of a lifetime.

As his personal centennial project, arts patron Floyd Chalmers commissioned an original opera about Louis Riel, the Métis rebel leader. At age twelve, Chalmers had been hired to distribute handbills for a touring show to every household in Orillia, Ontario. His reward was a fifty-cent payday, as well as a free ticket to the performance. He fell so deeply in love with the theatre that he later used the wealth he accumulated from running the Maclean-Hunter chain of magazines to support dramatic productions. He personally contributed $15,000 for the *Riel* project.

The new opera, one of two to be created for Centennial Year by the Canadian Opera Company—at an expense of nearly $500,000—featured music composed by Harry Somers. The bilingual libretto, believed to be the first ever created, was written by Mavor Moore, a dramatist and actor who had performed as Riel in an earlier theatre production. Moore had some assistance with the French-language parts from Montreal playwright Jacques Languirand.

An opera based on the life of Louis Riel revived interest in the Métis leader who had been hanged for his role in an 1885 rebellion. *Photo: Library and Archives Canada*

The title role fell to Bernard Joseph Roméo Vianney Turgeon, born in Edmonton to Noël, who was a cop, and Irene (née Robidas), who was an organist of note in her church. His father had French-Canadian roots, while his mother had some First Nations ancestry.

Turgeon had the build of a lumberjack, a rugged attractiveness and great physical strength. In order to play Riel, he grew a walrus moustache and donned a chequered jacket, tartan pants and a vest, with the colourful traditional Métis sash tied around his waist and dangling down his left leg. In the title role, he saw an opportunity to address a century-old injustice.

"You see, when I went to school in the West, Riel was dismissed as a rebel and an outlaw," Turgeon said. "This irritated my French blood. Now I'm not only getting a chance to sing the most difficult role in my career—you could compare it with Otello—but to help set history straight."

Riel was seen as a traitor by the English and as a martyr by the French. A visionary, an advocate for a people desiring only the right to self-rule, Riel found himself in conflict with the leaders of a fledgling nation: first in the Red River Rebellion of 1869 and 1870, and later in the Northwest Rebellion of 1885.

Opera Beyond Riel

Despite the profusion of Centennial Year events, Toronto mayor William Dennison managed to proclaim an Opera Month in the city, to honour the world premieres of *The Luck of Ginger Coffey* and *Louis Riel*, as well as the Canadian Opera Company's productions of *Il Trovatore*, *The Barber of Seville*, *The Tales of Hoffmann* and *Madama Butterfly*.

The Luck of Ginger Coffey was the Canadian Opera Company's other original work commissioned from Canadian artists on a Canadian theme for the Centennial. Written by Raymond Pannell and based upon Brian Moore's novel about a blatherskite Irishman's experiences as an immigrant, this work was dismissed by the *Star*'s Nathan Cohen as being "as colourless as *Riel* is colourful."

Another centennial initiative for the opera company was Prologue to the Performing Arts, in which volunteers brought capsule performances of operas to intermediate grade students at their schools.

Other operas written for centennial celebrations included *The Loyalists*, by Douglas Major; *Grant, Warden of the Plains*, by Murray Adaskin; *Sam Slick,* by Kelsey Jones; and *The Brideship*, by Robert Turner.

Benjamin Britten conducted the English Opera Group's performance of *The Beggar's Opera* as part of the World Festival of the Arts held at Place des Arts in Montreal. *Photo: Library and Archives Canada*

The opera captured sixteen years of the Manitoba schoolteacher's life, portrayed in eighteen scenes alternating between the rough West and the wood-panelled offices of dipsomaniacal prime minister Sir John A. Macdonald (portrayed by Dutch-born baritone Cornelis Opthof). The libretto included the actual prime ministerial statement, "He shall hang, though every dog in Quebec bark in his favour"—a verdict that nearly sundered a young nation and one which echoes to this day.

"Bernard Turgeon offers us a fair measure of Riel's messianic qualities, his ambition and his disturbed state of mind, plus a pretty heroic vocal performance," the critic William Littler told readers of the *Toronto Star*. The rival *Toronto Telegram* pronounced the show to be "big, efficient, exciting, heterogenous." The *New York Times* critic Raymond Ericson found much to admire. "Riel is shown in all his guises—self-doubting, hallucinating, unforgiving, courageous. Sir John, his great antagonist, comes to life as a political double-dealer and cynic. Bishop Taché, Riel's friend and supporter, is the sincere mediator betrayed all around." In the end, Ericson pronounced the opera's music too difficult to export.

The lead performer so inhabited this role of a lifetime that he sometimes seemed to have difficulty knowing where Riel ended and Turgeon began. "Some people close to the production felt at times that Turgeon was so involved in the role that he was confusing his own identity with Riel's," Ezra Schabas and Carl Morey wrote in *Opera Viva*, their history of the opera company. Turgeon's superb performance was praised as the production moved from its world premiere at the O'Keefe Centre in Toronto to Expo 67.

The *Riel* production was revived for six performances in 1968 and was adapted for television the following year, bringing Turgeon's performance to a wider audience. It was later revived at the Kennedy Center in Washington, DC, for American bicentennial celebrations in 1976.

In the course of his career, Turgeon performed before the Royal Family, a Canadian prime minister, and the presidents of Mexico and the United States. In retirement, he settled on Vancouver Island, where he operated Star Hill Farm with his wife Teresa, until his death in 2016. The farm, overlooking Elk Lake in suburban Saanich, outside Victoria, produced asparagus and rhododendrons.

Festival Canada: On the Move

A choreographed Inuit walrus hunt was one of the highlights of a two-hour performance by Les Feux Follets. Other indigenous dances from the Plains and the West Coast were also on the troupe's bill, as were jigs and reels and

A highlight of the touring Festival Canada shows was performances by Les Feux Follets, Montreal's renowned folk-dance troupe. *Photo: Boris Spremo / Toronto Star*

flings associated with the Acadian, Québécois, Scottish and Irish settlers of Eastern Canada.

The Montreal-based folk troupe included sixty-five dancers, singers and instrumentalists who presented the story of Canada in a show that toured the country before performing at the Canada pavilion at Expo 67. Les Feux Follets, whose name was usually translated as "Fireflies," brought to the stage the story of a nation and its peoples in song and dance.

The troupe's national tour was sponsored as part of Festival Canada, an ambitious program to bring the arts to the Canadian people. The National Youth Orchestra, the National Ballet of Canada (performing *The Nutcracker* and *La Sylphide*), and the New York Philharmonic, under the direction of conductor Leonard Bernstein, were among the many participating organizations to tour.

The children's theatre company Holiday Theatre, from Vancouver, entertained audiences from coast to coast. The Neptune Theatre, from Halifax, undertook its first transcontinental tour while presenting Sean O'Casey's *Juno and the Paycock* and *The Sleeping Bag*, a new comedy by Nova Scotia playwright Dr. Arthur L. Murphy. The latter involved a trio (two male scientists and a female secretary) awaiting rescue in the Arctic.

From its home in southwestern Ontario, the Stratford Festival Company toured with performances of Gogol's *The Government Inspector* and Shakespeare's *Twelfth Night*.

Jamie Ray (left) dances happily as the title character in *Anne of Green Gables: The Musical*, based on the classic tale by Lucy Maud Montgomery. The Charlottetown Festival production of *Anne of Green Gables* toured Canada for five weeks in 1967 under the auspices of Festival Canada. *Photo: Library and Archives Canada*

Under the direction of Sir Laurence Olivier, the National Theatre of Great Britain presented John Mortimer's version of *A Flea in Her Ear* and William Congreve's *Love in Canada*.

Canadians unable to get to Prince Edward Island in Centennial Year might have had PEI come to their hometown. The Confederation Centre Theatre of Charlottetown toured with its popular musical version of *Anne of Green Gables*.

Another famous regional theatre, based in the reconstructed British Columbia gold-rush town of Barkerville, presented vaudeville routines in a show called *The Best of Barkerville*.

Quebec's rich theatre scene was enlisted in Festival Canada, as Le Théâtre du Nouveau Monde, directed by Jean Gascon, presented Molière's *Le Bourgeois gentilhomme*, and Le Théâtre du Rideau Vert toured with *Terre d'Aube* by Jean-Paul Pinsonneault. A floating theatre known as Le Théâtre de l'Escale presented a varied repertoire as it docked at ports on the St. Lawrence River and throughout the Great Lakes.

Some of the Festival Canada programs got off to a slow start. Several Ontario centres originally rejected performances by Les Feux Follets, only to change their minds when early shows at the Lakehead received raves and sold-out crowds.

While the line-up favoured the formal arts, popular music received a nod as Festival Canada sponsored tours by the likes of folk singers The Travellers, and Ian and Sylvia. Don Messer and his Islanders, comprising some twenty-two artists, criss-crossed the land, bringing a down-home hoedown to halls across the country. The travelling show brought to small-town stages the acts familiar to a generation of television viewers: singer Marg Osbourne, Scottish crooner Johnny Forrest and jolly Charlie Chamberlain, a big man with a big grin, a bowler hat and a cane.

Caribana '67: Toronto's Festival

Toronto had never seen a parade like the mile-long procession snaking from Varsity Stadium toward City Hall in August. People dressed in colourful costumes danced along the route to steel drums and other musical sounds of the Caribbean diaspora.

To celebrate the Centennial, Toronto's West Indian community had kicked in their own money to organize a week-long festival called Caribana '67. Most events were held on Centre Island, the closest the ex-pats could get to finding a sandy venue in Toronto. Events included a kiddies' carnival, teen fashion shows, water-skiing demonstrations, cricket matches, steel orchestras, and a Caribbean-style folk-song championship lasting so long that the ferry back to the city ran long past midnight to get everyone home.

"The Centennial gave us an opportunity to give back something to this country," said Dr. J.A. Liverpool, who headed Caribana's board of directors. "No other cause could have united West Indians so completely. Politicians have failed in the past, but Canada has brought us all together."

Seven-year-old Chandra Galasso dances in a grass skirt on stage at Caribana '67 on Centre Island in Toronto. *Photo: Mario Geo / Toronto Star*

The poet and playwright Derek Walcott, who was born on Saint Lucia, attended Caribana as artistic director of the Trinidad Theatre Workshop that he had founded. "Everything in Trinidad explodes into an expression of art," he said, "but there is more to our culture than limbo dancing, calypso and steel bands. This is what we are out to prove." The company had a difficult debut in Toronto, as they had to perform outdoors on an open-air stage with only a canvas sheet as a backdrop. This was so disappointing that arrangements were quickly made to add indoor shows to the company's schedule. One of these shows was billed in newspapers as the world premiere of Walcott's *Dream on Monkey Mountain*. Walcott would be named a Nobel Laureate for literature in 1992.

Caribana was a bright spot on the calendar for a city in which some regretted not having challenged Montreal in bidding for a world's fair. "It's as if the West Indian community here came in to fill a vacuum in our own paltry centennial celebrations," the *Toronto Star* critic Antony Ferry wrote, "and taught us the art of enjoying an all-out fling." The celebration, now known formally as the Toronto Caribbean Carnival—though popularly as Caribana, continues to this day.

6 Military Moments

Saluting the Centennial in Style

CANADA'S MILITARY HAD done much to forge a sense of national identity in a young nation, showing bravery and tenacity on the battlefield in two world wars. The Centennial offered a chance to remind the Canadian people of the military's legacy. A national touring tattoo, an international assembly of friendly naval vessels and the creation of a short-lived aerial acrobatics team known as the Golden Centennaires brought the military to the people.

Major Tattoo

In the space of two hours and ten minutes, the Canadian Armed Forces Tattoo—a cross between a military parade and theatre—reviewed three hundred years of Canadian military history in a pageant of colourful costumes, booming cannons and stirring martial music. Vigorous performances entailed a nightly casualty rate of two, usually from scrapes or torn ligaments, a sustainable loss considering that the cast included as many as seventeen hundred performers.

"My idea of the show is a musical with color," said Brigadier Charles Peck, of Hillsboro, New Brunswick, chief of the defence department's centennial celebrations. The centennial tattoo was written, produced and directed by

TOP: The tattoo was a combination military parade and musical complete with a motor-cycle team and other entertainments. Two trains of tattoo performers criss-crossed the land in 1967, presenting a well-received spectacle telling the story of Canada's military. *Photo: Keith Wilson.* LEFT: A gun crew in red striped shirts demonstrates their skill for an audience attending one of the dress rehearsals for the military tattoo. *Photo: Keith Wilson.* RIGHT: All branches contributed to the Canadian Armed Forces Tattoo '67, portraying three centuries of armed forces history in Canada. Great research went into the uniforms to guarantee historical accuracy. *Photo: Keith Wilson*

Major Ian Fraser, of Pictou, Nova Scotia, of the Royal Highlanders of Canada (Black Watch). Previously, they had organized a tattoo for the Seattle World's Fair in 1962. The tattoo was an operation demanding military precision both in the staging and the performance. Two touring troupes of about 350 performers each travelled across the country by train, while organizers added one thousand extras to the cast for combined shows at Expo 67, the Pacific National Exhibition in Vancouver, and the Canadian National Exhibition in Toronto.

The desire for historical authenticity prompted officers to tour military museums in preparation for the show. The military purchased kilts from Scotland, replica French flintlocks from Belgium, and 150 Lee Enfield rifles with bayonets from an Australian source at $2.50 each. There were sabres, claymores, halberds, pikes and daggers.

A computer was called into service to assist in organizing two trains loaded with ninety tons of equipment. The largest productions called for nine hundred performers to undergo four costume changes nightly. There were a hundred fifers, pipers and drummers; five hundred other musicians; and more than three hundred others, including forty servicewomen, all of whose acts needed to be choreographed.

The retelling of Canada's military history began with a depiction of the arrival in 1665 of twelve hundred French regulars, comprising the Carignan-Salières regiment, and proceeded through the Battle of the Plains of Abraham to the Boer War, the World Wars, the Korean War and into the peacekeeping era.

A five-minute segment depicting men going "over the top" in a World War I battle had soldiers in khaki sprinting across a field only to flop as they ran, until a mere handful reached the other end. "The packed audience of 30,000 sits

Tap That Toe!

The word "tattoo" evolved from a seventeenth-century Dutch command. A drummer would be dispatched to inns and taverns to encourage soldiers to return to their billets. The order "tap toe!" ("taps shut!") was accompanied by a drum beat. This custom became a military parade through the streets. In English, "tap toe" was rendered as "taptoo," evolving into today's "tattoo."

silently with shock; suddenly the massed bands appear, and the spell of horror is broken," journalist Peter Worthington, himself a veteran of World War II and the Korean War, wrote in the *Toronto Telegram*. "It is the most eloquent condemnation imaginable of the futility and insanity of war."

Other segments included a motorcycle stunt act with up to ten men clinging to a machine; an Armed Forces Gymnastic Display Team of eighty tumblers; and "Drummer Boy's Dream of Half a Cake," depicting toy soldiers fighting over a piece of cake.

The insistence upon historical accuracy proved judicious. In the audience for the tour's opening performance at Peterborough, Ontario, was John Pilling, a Boer War veteran.

"Even in the more desultory historical sequences, the actors show swash-buckling military verve—whether playing Indian lacrosse, disporting with camp followers, or merely clutching a Bible," noted *Time Magazine*.

come in, BiRD DOG:

As part of a training mission, the Canadian Army Signal Corps decided to send a commemorative centennial message across Canada using all techniques employed by the corps during its history. The mission was named Project Mercury '67.

On June 27, British Columbia Lieutenant-Governor George Pearkes spoke into a microphone at the Legislature in Victoria, his voice carried by laser beam to the Fleet Mail Room at Canadian Forces Base (CFB) Esquimalt. The message was then conveyed by mail to Vancouver, where it was communicated by teletype to Winnipeg and then by radio to CFB Petawawa, outside Ottawa. A Cessna L-19 Bird Dog dropped the message to a canoe party on the Ottawa River, which took it to Parliament Hill. A telephone call to CFB St. Hubert in Quebec continued the message's eastward progress. Radio relay, a field telephone, a Fullerphone, and dispatch riders on jeeps, motorcycles, a ferry and a horse transmitted the message to Bedford, Nova Scotia. From there, a heliograph, a Lucas lamp and signal flags took the message to Halifax Citadel, where a submarine cable relayed it to St. John's, after which a semaphore and a Lucas lamp passed the message to a runner, who carried it up Signal Hill on Dominion Day morning to a waiting Fabien O'Dea, the lieutenant-governor of Newfoundland. His reply was conveyed to his vice-regal counterpart later in the day.

The tattoo's success sparked a public demand that it be exported as an expression of the nation, like the Red Army Chorus of the Soviet Union, or the Blue Angels aerial acrobatics team of the United States. Impresario Sol Hurok expressed interest in touring the show, but said he had been told that the prime minister had vetoed the idea.

Centennial Naval Assembly

It was the largest assembly of ships to gather in Canada in peacetime. The forty-ship armada that came together in Halifax in June for the Centennial Naval Assembly included vessels from sixteen nations that ranged in size from the Italian sailing yacht *Corsaro II* to the Canadian replenishment ship *Provider*, a 22,000-ton behemoth. The largest fighting ship in the fleet was the American cruiser *Newport News*. Some 23,000 sailors were involved.

Governor General Roland Michener reviewed the moored ships from the minesweeper *Chaleur,* with three RCMP patrol vessels as an escort. Afterward, he ordered Canadian sailors to "splice the main brace" in recognition of the assembly—which meant an extra tot of rum was granted in honour of a special occasion. The command referred to the old act of splicing a piece of rigging, an onerous task that traditionally was rewarded with rum.

Golden Centennaires Take Off

The Tutors streaked across the sky, a six-plane wedge in striking livery, with a gold upper surface and a dark blue underside separated by a red stripe. A winged centennial symbol was painted below the cockpit. The formation was known as a "Double Delta."

The aerial acrobatics of the Royal Canadian Air Force team thrilled audiences at a hundred centennial demonstrations, from Expo 67 all the way to the Abbotsford Air Show in British Columbia.

The squad had been formed to mark the national centennial, as well as the fiftieth anniversary of military aviation in Canada. The Centennaires took to the skies only three years after their predecessors, the Golden Hawks, had been disbanded as a cost-cutting measure.

By using the Montreal-built Canadair Tutors, jet trainers with high manoeuvrability, Wing Commander O.B. Philp figured that the Centennaires could create a program that did not involve the long waits required for high-powered jets to get back into position for follow-up stunts.

The Golden Centennaires thrilled audiences with their daring aerial acrobatics in shows across the country, including the opening of Expo 67. This CT-114 Tutor, displayed in the team's brilliant livery, is on display at Portage la Prairie, Manitoba. *Photo: Bill Zuk*

POLAR DELIVERY

In November 1967, a twenty-five-man crew aboard a Yukon aircraft attached to No. 412 Squadron, Air Transport Command decided to mark a marathon training mission by dropping a centennial flag on the North Pole.

The honour of dispatching the flag while flying at nearly 9,500 metres fell to Corporal L.L. McMillan, a twenty-six-year-old from Victoria, British Columbia, who braved an outside temperature of a numbing minus 59.4 degrees Celsius before heaving the flag.

The plane left the air force base at Uplands, near Ottawa, and travelled 49,600 kilometres in ninety-one hours, with stopovers in Alaska, Hawaii, New Zealand, Australia and Guam. And one delivery at the North Pole.

THE YEAR CANADIANS LOST THEIR MINDS AND FOUND THEIR COUNTRY

"This, to my mind, was what we needed to accomplish—something different, distinctive and uniquely Canadian," Philp recorded in his memoir, part of which was published in *A Tradition of Excellence: Canada's Airshow Team Heritage*. The aim, Philp said, was to please the public with a "safe, albeit spectacular, well-choreographed show."

Philp and Squadron Leader C.B. Lang, who admired European teams, devised a show comprising the best of American power and European skill for a uniquely Canadian take on aerial acrobatics.

The pilots recruited to the team, which would be known jocularly as Philp's Flying Circus, needed flying skill and an ability to communicate with the public. They'd also have to have the kind of personality conducive to living alongside teammates in a pressure-packed nine-month assignment. Sixteen slots for pilots were filled from among seventy-six volunteer applicants.

The Golden Centennaires shows included eight Tutors, a Voodoo, a Starfighter and a Silver Star, as well as a pair of Avro 540K open-cockpit biplanes of World War I vintage. The Avros were in disrepair and needed to be rebuilt with parts found across the country, including original wheels that had been spotted on a farmer's cart. As the biplanes would not be able to fly back and forth across the country for performances, they had their wings removed after a show and were flown by a C-130 Hercules transport.

Two pilots were killed in training sessions: Tom Bebb and Dave Barker. The former had designed the winged shield that became the team emblem, while the latter had devised the solo acrobatics regarded as one of the most exciting parts of the show. Their deaths were a reminder to the other pilots of the risks inherent in the demonstration.

The Centennaires were disbanded after that year. The tradition of air force acrobatic teams would be revived in 1971 with the formation of the Snowbirds.

escapers' helpers

As a centennial project, the RCAF Escaping Society, a band of airmen who had evaded capture by the Germans in occupied Europe thanks to partisans and sympathizers, brought fifteen escapers' helpers to Canada for reunions with the men whom they had saved.

Sports

A Shining Year for Athletes

Centennial Year was a great time to be a Canadian sports fan. The national hockey team, comprised of amateurs—most of them university students—knocked off the Soviets to win a hockey tournament. Canadians won gold at the Pan Am Games in a flash (the 100-metre dash) and over the long haul (the marathon). Provincial teams competed in canoes across the Prairies and the Canadian Shield, retracing the route of the voyageurs in a race to the site of Expo 67. A series of peaks in the Yukon was conquered. In the professional arena, the Toronto Maple Leafs won the coveted Stanley Cup for the fourth time in six years. Their fans undoubtedly expected many more championships to come.

Pan Ams Come to Canada

The largest sporting event ever held in North America opened in Winnipeg in the summer of Centennial Year. The Manitoba capital was host to the fifth Pan American Games, the Olympics of the Western Hemisphere, attracting 2,400 athletes from twenty-eight nations.

After fallow years at international sporting competitions, Canadian athletes benefitted from their first Pan Am home-field advantage, claiming ninety-two medals, including twelve golds. The sprinter Harry Jerome of Vancouver

ABOVE: Andy Boychuk celebrates his Pan Am Games marathon victory on the podium with runners-up Agustín Calle of Colombia (left) and Alfredo Peñaloza of Mexico. *Photo: Library and Archives Canada.* FACING PAGE, TOP: Montreal weightlifter Pierre St-Jean won a bronze medal at the Pan Am Games. He also competed in three Olympics. *Photo: Library and Archives Canada.* BOTTOM: Teenaged swimmer Elaine Tanner, nicknamed Mighty Mouse, signs an autograph for a young fan at the Pan Am Games. *Photo: Library and Archives Canada*

needed only ten seconds to win his gold medal, while marathoner Andy Boychuk of Oshawa, Ontario, needed 2 hours, 23 minutes and 2.3 seconds to win his. Shot-putter Nancy McCredie began the games in a hospital bed with an inflamed knee, though she recovered in time to make a toss of 49 feet, 9¾ inches. She had dropped considerable weight and had eliminated food supplements from her diet. "The loss of the excess baggage has been easier on my knees, has helped me to increase my speed and [to] develop a better style," said McCredie, who was from the Toronto neighbourhood of Don Mills.

Three more gold medals were won in the pool, as sixteen-year-old Elaine Tanner, Canada's "Mighty Mouse" from Vancouver, won two backstroke sprints. Ralph Hutton, from the company town of Ocean Falls, British Columbia, took the men's 200-metre backstroke.

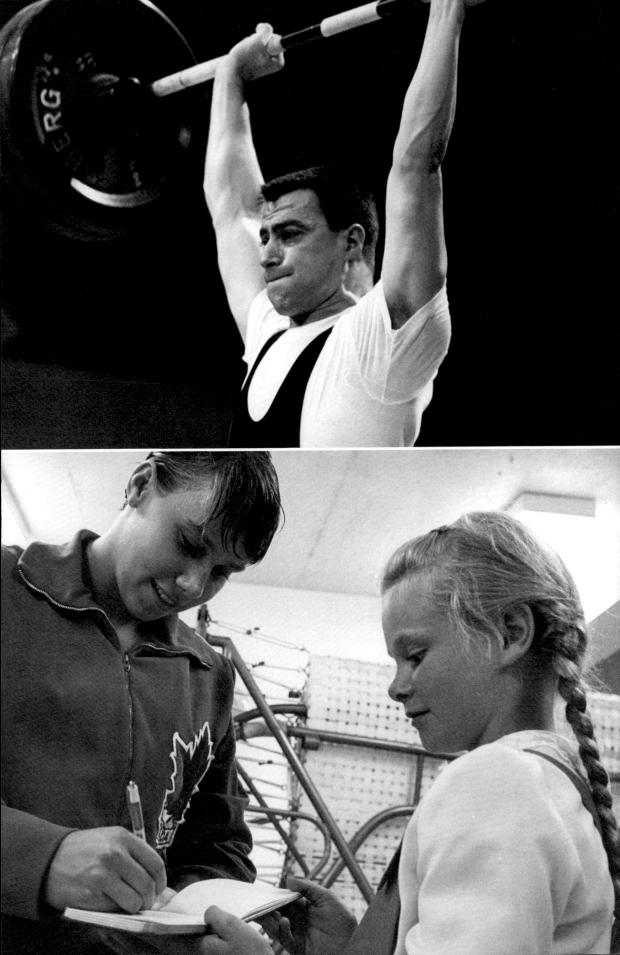

Pan am Games Standings

	GOLD	SILVER	BRONZE
United States	120	63	44
Canada	12	37	43
Brazil	11	10	5
Argentina	9	14	11
Cuba	8	14	23
Mexico	5	14	24
Trinidad-Tobago	2	3	3
Venezuela	1	4	5
Colombia	1	2	5
Puerto Rico	1	1	4
Chile	1	1	3

Peru (0, 2, 1), Uruguay (0, 1, 4), Panama (0, 1, 3), Ecuador (0, 1, 2), Bermuda (0, 1, 1), Barbados (0, 1, 0), Jamaica (0, 0, 3), Guyana (0, 0, 1), Netherlands Antilles (0, 0, 1)

ABOVE: An aerial view of a new stadium built for the Pan American Games on the University of Manitoba campus. The Opening and Closing Ceremonies as well as track and field events were held at the stadium. *Photo: University of Manitoba Archives & Special Collections.* FACING PAGE, TOP: A driving rain failed to dampen the enthusiasm of Prince Philip and the crowd in attendance for the Opening Ceremonies of the Pan American Games in Winnipeg. *Photo: University of Manitoba Archives & Special Collections.* BOTTOM LEFT: Wheelchair sports came to the Pan American Games in 1967 when six nations competed at the Paraplegic Games, which opened on August 8. The competing nations were Canada, Mexico, Jamaica, Argentina, the United States, and Trinidad and Tobago. *Photo: University of Manitoba Archives & Special Collections.* BOTTOM RIGHT: Bill Toomey, of Philadelphia, won the decathlon at the Pan American Games. A year later, he took gold at the Mexico City Olympics in the same gruelling, ten-sport event. *Photo: University of Manitoba Archives & Special Collections*

Other golds were won by Doug Rogers of Vancouver, an airplane pilot, and Michael Johnson of Hamilton, Ontario, in judo. Susan McDonnell of Toronto was the champion of the uneven bars, while Alf Mayer of Kitchener, Ontario, outshot the competition in English match rifle. The 150-kilometre road race was taken by Marcel Roy of Lac Megantic, Quebec. On the final day of competition, Jim Day of King, Ontario, won the individual equestrian jumping title aboard Canadian Club, a chestnut gelding. At first, Day thought he had lost a showdown against a Brazilian rival. "You could have knocked me for a loop when I'd heard I won," he said afterwards. "I was reading the clock backwards."

Prairie hospitality gave the Games a friendly atmosphere, though the occasional Cold War tensions flared. A gathering of athletes at the Winnipeg Arena prior to marching into the adjacent stadium for the Opening Ceremonies was interrupted when Cuban athletes started chanting, *"Cuba nunca se rinde"* ("Cuba never surrenders"). The Americans responded with hissing. Tensions eased after Mexican athletes convinced the Cubans to lead the gathering in song.

Prince Philip officially opened the Games during a downpour. Also in attendance were Prime Minister Lester Pearson and Premier Duff Roblin, who was in the midst of an unsuccessful campaign to become federal Conservative leader. The Cubans were cheered during the opening Parade of Nations for waving little Canadian flags that they had hidden in their pockets. They wore bright red berets befitting revolutionaries. Sandy Gilchrist, a swimmer from Ocean Falls, read the athlete's oath before one thousand pigeons were released to signify peace.

The male athletes were housed at an army base, while the female athletes were scattered throughout the city. One of the charming features of the Games was the sharing of events. The small farming town of Carman, south of Winnipeg near the border with North Dakota, played host to a Pan Am baseball game. Other baseball games were held in Portage la Prairie, while the final match, won by the United States over Cuba, 2-1, in the bottom of the ninth with one out, was played at Winnipeg Stadium.

As expected, the United States dominated the competition, winning gold in 120 of 170 events. Countries that competed but failed to win a medal included the Bahamas, El Salvador, Guatemala, Paraguay, Nicaragua, Costa Rica, Bolivia and the Virgin Islands.

The Pan Am Paraplegic Games began a week after the Closing Ceremonies.

The Games left Winnipeg with several outstanding sporting facilities. The University of Manitoba stadium boasted a million-dollar all-weather track,

Ten teams of ten paddlers raced in the Centennial Voyageur Canoe Pageant, a 104-day, 5,283-kilometre journey. *Photo: Library and Archives Canada*

and the $2.7-million Pan Am Pool was rated among the top three in the world, boasting Canada's only ten-metre diving tower at the time. The indoor velodrome was designed to be home also to amateur football in the city. A $40,000 venue for gymnastics, paid for by residents of the Winnipeg suburb of St. James, was used as a civic centre after the Games.

The Pan Am Games would return to Winnipeg in 1999, by which time the number of events and competitors would have nearly doubled.

Canoeing: 104-day Pageant

They pushed off from the starting line, ten teams carving paddles into the high waters of the swollen North Saskatchewan River, on which ice still floated in May. A pouring rain drenched the dignitaries on the shore, including Secretary of State Judy LaMarsh and Alberta Lieutenant-Governor Grant MacEwan. Participants in the Centennial Voyageur Canoe Pageant were making the first of an estimated four million strokes needed to finish a 104-day, 5,283-kilometre odyssey through five provinces to Expo 67 in Montreal.

The Centennial Voyageur Canoe Pageant pitted eight provincial and two territorial teams in a canoe race across the prairies and the Canadian Shield, including arduous portages. Each canoe was named for a famed explorer. *Photo: Superior National Forest / Flickr*

Jesuits Join in

At North Bay, Ontario, the centennial voyageurs were joined by four canoes propelled by twenty-four young Jesuits, most of them seminarians. They retraced the canoe route used by seventeenth-century missionaries. They launched their journey at Midland, the Ontario site of the Martyrs' Shrine dedicated to the murdered members of the Society of Jesus.

The Jesuits and their guests are scheduled to make a Canadian Canoe Pilgrimage in the summer of 2017, to promote reconciliation among the First Nat ions and the English and French peoples of Canada. The voyage is expected to follow the eastern shore of Georgian Bay to the French River, then to Lake Nipissing and on to the Mattawa, Ottawa and St. Lawrence Rivers to Montreal.

Three years of planning resulted in a route retracing the path of the original voyageurs through the unforgiving landscape of the Canadian Shield and the Prairies. The teams represented the two territories and eight of the ten provinces, with Newfoundland and Prince Edward Island sitting out the competition.

The route included 113 kilometres of arduous portaging, some days demanding fourteen hours of paddling. Each team had ten members, with six in the canoe at any one time. The youngest paddler was seventeen, the oldest fifty-two. They paddled canoes with the centennial symbol on the bow, each named for an explorer: *Samuel de Champlain* (New Brunswick), *John Cabot* (Nova Scotia), *La Vérendrye* (Quebec) and *Alexander Mackenzie* (Northwest Territories) among them.

To get started, the first day entailed only a 77-kilometre course from Rocky Mountain House to Alder Flats, Alberta. The third day ended in Edmonton, where the canoeists met the Queen's cousin, Princess Alexandra, and her husband, Angus Ogilvy. The voyageurs continued onward, through torrential rains and unrelenting prairie sun, maddening biting insects in Northern Ontario and the sapping humidity of Eastern Canada. By June 1, they would be at Lloydminster on the Alberta–Saskatchewan border; by July 1, at Winnipeg; by August 11, at Sault Ste. Marie.

VOYAGEUR STANDINGS

Manitoba: 507 hours, 21 minutes, 51 seconds

(Chief Voyageur: Jim Rheaume; Captain: Norm Crerar; Crew members: Roger Carriere, Blair Harvey, Gib McEachern, Joe Michelle, John Norman, Wayne Soltys, Don Starkell, David Wells)

British Columbia: 509:41.55

Alberta: 511:33.45

Followed by (in order of finish): Ontario, New Brunswick, Saskatchewan, Quebec, Northwest Territories, Yukon, Nova Scotia.

The cross-country centennial race was suggested in 1964 by Gene Rheaume, a Métis social worker who was the Progressive Conservative member of Parliament for the Northwest Territories. He passed the idea on to his brother, Jim, and to Norm Tyson, who had taken part in organizing the three-day canoe sprints featured in the annual Gold Rush Canoe Derby at Flin Flon, Manitoba. Marathon canoe racing had become popular on the northern plains in the mid-1960s, with a major brewery offering sponsorship and prize money.

On August 29, the voyageurs arrived in Ottawa, where Centennial Commissioner John Fisher described them as "harbingers of the centennial" for having visited hamlets along a water route across the continent. They traversed such waterways as Cedar Lake, Lake Winnipegosis, Lake Manitoba, Assiniboine River, Red River, Lake Winnipeg, Winnipeg River, Lake of the Woods, Rainy River, Lake Superior, Lake Nipissing, the Ottawa River, and, at long last, the St. Lawrence. The longest portage extended more than thirty kilometres, from Delta at the south end of Lake Manitoba to Portage la Prairie, a tough distance to haul a canoe weighing 118 kilograms.

In Ottawa, the canoeists were treated like conquering heroes, as some seven thousand spectators cheered their arrival at Britannia Bay. At a banquet that night, the agriculture minister praised the canoeists for their physiques. "After

Centennial Tournament Stats

	GP	W	L	GF	GA	PTS
Canada	3	3	0	17	8	6
Czechoslovakia	3	2	1	16	9	4
Soviet Union	3	1	2	13	11	2
United States	3	0	3	4	22	0

Dec. 31, 1966	Canada	5	Czechoslovakia	3
Jan. 1, 1967	Soviet Union	7	United States	1
Jan. 3	Canada	7	United States	1
Jan. 4	Czechoslovakia	5	Soviet Union	2
Jan. 5	Czechoslovakia	8	United States	2
Jan. 6	Canada	5	Soviet Union	4

seeing so many of these flabby fellows around Parliament Hill," Joe Greene said, according to the *Ottawa Journal*, "it's good to see there are still some rugged Canadians around."

The Manitoba crew recorded the fastest accumulated time, finishing in 507 hours, 21 minutes and 51 seconds, more than two hours ahead of the crew from British Columbia. The winners claimed a purse of $2,500 each, not counting the many smaller prizes awarded for sprints at the end of some legs of the race. The crew, most of them from Flin Flon, were inducted into the Manitoba Sports Hall of Fame in 2010.

The crew members of the *Alexander Mackenzie* were inducted into the Northwest Territories Sport Hall of Fame in 2012, despite having finished eighth in the race. The slowest team, from Nova Scotia, needed more than 542 hours to complete the journey.

The Albertan team's canoe, named after David Thompson, is on display today at the Rocky Mountain House Historical Site.

Hockey: Centennial Cup

Prime Minister Lester Pearson was among the patrons at a sold-out Winnipeg Arena on January 6 when the Canadian national hockey team came from behind to defeat the Soviet Union, 5–4. The defeat of the defending world champions gave Canada the championship of the four-team, round-robin Centennial World Invitational Tournament. Pearson stepped on the ice after the game to present a trophy to Canadian captain Roger Bourbonnais.

Later, Pearson reflected upon his feelings at that moment: "When they ran up that flag, the teams lined up opposite each other, and we all sang 'O Canada'. . . then I knew what the definition of a Canadian is."

The victory was a rare success for Canada in an era when the nation had unhappily surrendered its crown as a hockey powerhouse, a title lost as amateurs found themselves competing against Soviet and Czech athletes who were professional in all but name.

Reverend David Bauer, the architect of the national team, filled the roster with exemplary young men, all university students. Under coach Jackie McLeod, Canada defeated the Czechs by 5–3 before swamping the Americans by 7–1. (The lone American goal was scored, unassisted, by Bill Masterton, who would die a year later after suffering a head injury in a National Hockey League game.) The Soviet game was a see-saw affair, with the visitors enjoying leads of 2–0 and 3–1. Defenceman Carl Brewer, a former professional, scored a key

A ski jumper soars down a slope near Quebec City during the inaugural Canada Winter Games. *Photo: Library and Archives Canada*

goal for Canada. Billy MacMillan scored the winner in the third period, with goalie Wayne Stephenson foiling subsequent Soviet attacks.

The Canadian team went on to win the bronze medal at the 1968 Winter Olympics.

Canada Winter Games

An amateur sports meet for Canadians was first proposed in 1924, but the idea did not come to fruition until the Centennial Commission decided that the Winter Games should be held in 1967. Under the slogan "Unity through sport," more than eighteen hundred athletes gathered in Quebec City to compete in such sports as skiing, ski jumping, speed skating, figure skating, shooting, hockey, wrestling, volleyball, basketball, gymnastics and badminton.

On the opening day, February 11, the thermometer dropped forty degrees during the day, to minus thirty-three Celsius. Continued poor weather forced the schedule to be revised, after a blizzard dumped seventy-six centimetres of snow on the city.

Despite some planning glitches—such as officials scrambling at the last minute to find a torch to light the cauldron for the flame that would burn during the Winter Games—the event was considered a success.

Doreen McCannell, a nineteen-year-old university student from Winnipeg, won four gold medals in speed skating. She later competed at three Winter Olympics. The men's figure-skating champion was seventeen-year-old Toller Cranston, who would become a legend in the sport. The prime minister handed out medals to the gymnasts.

Don MacLeod, an Olympic cross-country skier, pops a paper bag to start the Centennial Ski Marathon in the Montreal suburb of Pointe-Claire. The race is still held annually. *Photo: Canadian Ski Museum*

The hockey tournament was won by the University of Alberta Golden Bears, led by Brian Harper, the younger brother of NHL defenceman Terry Harper. Alberta defeated the University of British Columbia Thunderbirds 4-1 in the final.

Ontario topped the standings, followed by British Columbia and Alberta.

The Canada Games have been held every two years since, with alternating summer and winter competitions. More than one hundred thousand young athletes, including Bruny Surin, Steve Nash and Clara Hughes, have taken part over the years.

Skiing: Centennial Marathon

Don MacLeod, a member of Canada's national ski team, organized a cross-country skiing marathon between Montreal and Ottawa. About four hundred skiers, aged from five to ninety-two—the latter the famed "Jackrabbit" Johannsen—took part in the three-day event, though only a fraction skied the entire distance of 160 kilometres (one hundred miles; one mile for each year of Confederation).

After starting at a suburban shopping centre outside Montreal, the tour's first day ended at Lachute, Quebec; the second at Plantagenet, Ontario, and the third at the train station converted into the Centennial Centre in downtown Ottawa, with the marathoners joined by other skiers on the Rideau Canal into the city.

The Canadian Ski Marathon continues to this day—a popular, two-day event through beautiful, snowy countryside. The skiers who complete the run while wearing packs and sleeping outdoors overnight qualify for the title "Coureur des bois."

Mountain Climbing

YUKON ALPINE EXPEDITION

The largest mountaineering expedition in history sought to challenge a series of unclimbed peaks in Canada's highest and wildest range. The Saint Elias Mountains were majestic, isolated and, until 1967, untouched. The Yukon Alpine Centennial Expedition, organized by the Alpine Club of Canada, attracted applications from more than three hundred mountaineers vying to participate in attempts to conquer the peaks (later known as the Centennial Range).

The expedition was designed to express national pride and achievement, while also focusing on the co-operative nature of mountain climbing—when one's life depends upon the actions of the others to whom one is tethered.

For stage one, the lead was shared by a Canadian (English-born Monty Alford, of the Yukon) and an American (Vin Hoeman, of Anchorage, a Kentucky-born climber who would die in an avalanche in Nepal two years later). Their team of eight climbers formed a joint expedition to mark the centennials of Confederation and of the Alaska Purchase by tackling the south summit of Mount Vancouver, which would be named Good Neighbour Peak. Co-leader Alford wrote for the *Canadian Alpine Journal*, "One felt so completely isolated. With other massifs made to look like islands as they penetrated the sun-drenched canopy, the scene was breathtaking." The team planted two national flags and a centennial flag at the summit.

Next, fifty-two climbers, in thirteen four-member teams, attempted to reach the tops of peaks that had been named for the ten provinces and two territories. A final peak in the range was to be named "Centennial" in honour of Canada's anniversary. Climbers were ferried to high glacier bases by helicopter. The climbs were challenging and the conditions less than ideal, as snow and ice hampered even some reconnaissance missions. Despite the hardships, eleven teams planted centennial flags on summits. Centennial Peak resisted three attempts, but was conquered on the fourth.

Mount Manitoba thwarted a team led by Paddy Sherman, the English-born Vancouver newspaperman.

Fifteen years later, the summit was at last reached, when veteran climber Peter Aitchison, a mathematics professor (who later died in a climbing accident), led a team from Manitoba with his son, Jeff.

An all-woman team—Gertrude Smith, of Vancouver; Helen Butling of Nelson, British Columbia; and Wendy Teichmann and Andrea Rankin, both of Montreal—had to call off their climb on Mount Saskatchewan because of poor conditions. They were within 274 metres of the summit of the 3,342-metre peak. "We were hampered by low cloud, blizzard conditions and mild weather and poor snow conditions," said Gertrude Smith. "The snow . . . just slipped off the ice, which made it very dangerous." She added that the team was reluctant to call off the attempt lest their failure be attributed to their gender. "I feel we should go again and do it with an all-woman team, to show them we can do it." Subsequent attempts by other climbers—in 2005, on the centennial of Saskatchewan's becoming a province; in 2007; and in 2012—also failed.

One climber, Roland Reader of Ottawa, who had taken part in the successful scaling of Mount Ontario, stayed in the area, though he had to be evacuated after breaking a leg while skiing across a glacier.

Expedition members named many features in their climbs, and also observed the sparse, desperate life at such altitudes. An academic study has since shown that many of the mountaineers were motivated less by nationalism than by an interest in exploring their relationship with the natural world. Their climbs contributed to the creation of the Kluane National Park and Reserve, which encompasses the Centennial Range.

A moment of levity occurred when Judy LaMarsh, wearing boots and parka, visited the expedition's general camp on a grassy area at Steele Glacier. After being flown by helicopter near the summit of a nearby peak, the indefatigable secretary of state could not resist the impulse to attempt a yodel.

ERIK SHEER, PRETEEN EXTRAORDINAIRE

A freckle-faced boy with blond hair and blue eyes announced a centennial project as ambitious as it was daunting. The ten-year-old planned to ascend snow-capped Mount Kilimanjaro, Africa's highest peak, to publicize Canada's birthday and the world's fair. That the lad had a lean, even frail, build made his attempted conquest all the more unlikely.

George Armstrong led his Toronto Maple Leafs to a surprise upset of the Montreal Canadiens to claim the Stanley Cup in six games in 1967. *Photo: Library and Archives Canada*

Erik Sheer—what a family name for a mountaineer!—became accustomed to climbing hills after learning to ski at the age of two. The Ottawa boy regularly tackled Mount Marcy in the Adirondacks with his father, Frank Sheer, a civil servant. The boy described the 1,629-metre Marcy climb as "a cinch." But Kilimanjaro is nearly four times as high.

The Centennial Commission promised to give Erik two hundred pennants, a hundred Canadian flags and a centennial flag to be planted at the peak. The Alberta town of St. Paul gave him a microfilm of their centennial projects—including a landing pad for flying saucers—to be screened for an audience of Tanzanians. The mayor of Ottawa gave him a letter to present to his counterpart in Dar es Salaam.

When not planning the conquest of a continent's tallest peak, the boy collected coins and comics, stamps and matchboxes, postcards and tourist pamphlets. He played hockey, baseball, football and soccer. He also liked to read mysteries.

Raising money for the project presented a problem. Because the event was to take place outside Canada, the Centennial Commission would not cover any costs incurred. And since the project was designed to promote Canada, the boy's father did not wish to accept any donations from Americans.

Newspaper stories generated interest from some companies, which then provided footgear, sleeping bags and dehydrated food. One donated a small dictating machine, which Erik planned to use to record his impressions, for possible future use on a CBC Radio program about his adventure.

Father and son appeared on Tanzania Day at Expo 67, where they were presented with a Tanzanian flag.

They were accompanied on their ascent by Dr. Michael Wiedman, a Boston physician whom they had met on one of their numerous Adirondack climbs. The doctor decided to join them in Africa to monitor the effect of high altitude and poor conditions on the boy's health. ("I feel a lot safer having a doctor along," Erik's father acknowledged.)

After arriving in Africa but before beginning their climb, the group attended the funeral of a twenty-seven-year-old Austrian alpine guide who had died after becoming lost on the mountain. Frank Sheer was surprised to see two graves dug when only one body was to be buried. He was told that the extra hole was for the mountain's next victim, whoever that might be.

The party began the five-day ascent in good spirits, but soon were bogged down in snow and mud. Erik refused to be carried, though he found the slog arduous. "He went on and cried and went on and cried," his father said. "He cried himself up the mountain."

At the 16,000-foot level, the party faced snow so deep that it was nearly twice the boy's height. The guide refused to continue, and the group returned to camp.

"I really couldn't care less about a record," Erik told reporters after returning to Ottawa. "Our purpose was just to climb. But we ran into snow four to seven feet deep and that's too deep for me." He stood just four feet eight inches tall.

The flags intended for the peak were given instead to the Canadian High Commission, for presentation to Tanzanian president Julius Nyerere.

Father and son pledged a second assault on Kilimanjaro.

As a young man, Erik continued to climb mountains. In 1978, he participated in a month-long expedition through the isolated Torngat Mountains on the northern tip of Newfoundland and Labrador. He joined Ron Parker and Ray Chipeniuk in becoming the first Canadians to climb the 1,652-metre Mount Caubvick (also known as Mont d'Iberville). The youngest of the trio impressed his partners with his skill.

"He had great natural ability," Chipeniuk said recently. "He was formidable in getting over a landscape of very broken rock. He skipped from boulder to boulder to cross sizeable streams. Always cheerful, always game to take things on."

The following year, Sheer was working in Norway, where his maternal grandparents lived. On June 19, he was killed in a motorcycle accident on the highway. He was twenty-one years old.

His mountaineering friends named a spectacular ravine in the Torngat the "Sheer Couloir." As they told the *Canadian Alpine Journal*, "We imagine Erik's spirit standing watch in that malachite-encrusted cockpit at the top of the gully."

Sheer had taken 415 photographic slides on his Torngat expedition. These were donated after his death by his father to Memorial University, where they now can be found in the archives of the Labrador Institute—a final, lasting contribution to mountaineering in the land he loved.

On Other Sports Fronts

Curling: The Parkway team skippered by Alf Phillips Jr. won the Macdonald Brier Tankard for Ontario, beating Manitoba in a tournament held in Ottawa. The other members of his rink were John Ross, Ron Manning and Keith Reilly. Betty Duguid's Fort Garry rink claimed the Canadian Ladies' Curling championship held in Montreal. Her team members were Joan Ingram, Laurie Bradawaski and Dot Rose.

Football: Canadian football's Grey Cup championship game was held in the nation's capital at Lansdowne Park, with the Hamilton Tiger-Cats defeating the defending champion Saskatchewan Roughriders, 24-1. Bobby Gimby was the star of the half-time show with a rendition of "Canada," his smash

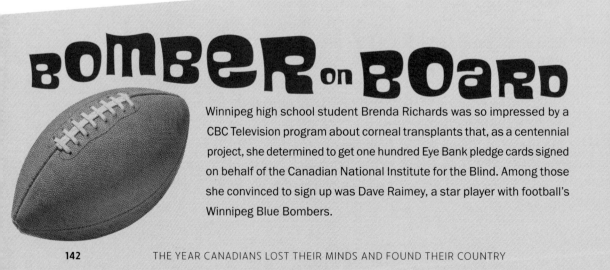

BOMBER on BOARD

Winnipeg high school student Brenda Richards was so impressed by a CBC Television program about corneal transplants that, as a centennial project, she determined to get one hundred Eye Bank pledge cards signed on behalf of the Canadian National Institute for the Blind. Among those she convinced to sign up was Dave Raimey, a star player with football's Winnipeg Blue Bombers.

centennial hit. The Tiger-Cats wore special helmets that season, with a leaping tiger appearing over a red centennial symbol.

Hockey: The Drummondville Eagles swept the Calgary Spurs in four games played in Quebec to claim the Allan Cup, representing senior hockey supremacy. The Toronto Marlboros defeated the Port Arthur (Ontario) Marrs in six games, all in the Lakehead, to win the Memorial Cup as the best in junior hockey. The Marlies' roster included a young defenceman named Brad Park, a future Hockey Hall of Fame inductee. With an empty-net goal in the final minute of play, thirty-six-year-old Toronto Maple Leafs captain George Armstrong assured a win for Toronto at Maple Leaf Gardens over the archrival Montréal Canadiens. The victory gave the Leafs the Stanley Cup, as professional hockey champions for the fourth time in six seasons. (The National Hockey League would be adding six new American franchises for the next season, doubling in size.) The Leafs later paraded up Bay Street to City Hall in open convertibles.

Lacrosse: The Vancouver Carlings defeated the Brooklin (Ontario) Redmen in six games, to claim the Mann Cup as Canadian senior lacrosse champions. The Oshawa (Ontario) Green Gaels continued their dominance of junior lacrosse by once again claiming the Minto Cup. The New Westminster (British Columbia) Junior Salmonbellies were their victims for a fourth consecutive season.

Running: Hazel Oakley of Toronto was credited as the first woman to complete a 100-mile (160-kilometre) centennial run, a physical fitness project launched nationally by the YMCA. In an era when women were forbidden from entering competitions such as the Boston Marathon, Oakley accumulated her total in runs of one, two or three miles every day over two months. The thirty-six-year-old homemaker was the mother of two and was married to a man stationed at the air force base at Saint-Hubert, Quebec. The Montreal Businessman's Health Club pledged to run a combined 100,000 miles by July 1 and challenged other clubs across the land to match the total. Prime Minister Lester Pearson joined runners at the outset on Parliament Hill in January.

Ski-jumping: A twenty-nine-year-old housepainter from Sweden won the Canadian Centennial Ski Jump Meet at Camp Fortune, north of Gatineau, Quebec. Kjell Sjöberg endured sub-zero temperatures and gusty winds to outjump thirty-four competitors, winning the individual title before two thousand chilled spectators. The team championship was won by Czechoslovakia, followed by Sweden, Austria, Switzerland, the United States, Japan and Canada. Ivar Frederiksen was the top Canadian, with a twelfth-place finish. Other Canadian jumpers were Jacques Charland, Rhéal Séguin and Pat Morris, a junior. A grant of $16,900 from the Canadian Amateur Ski Association facilitated the event, the largest of its kind ever held in Canada.

School Fitness Tests

One morning in January 1967, in Ottawa, fourteen students aged between seven and seventeen gathered to undergo a physical test. They were to be judged in the three mandatory challenges of the Centennial Commission's sports award program.

The boys and girls had to perform a standing broad jump, speed sit-ups for one minute, and a three-hundred-yard run done in bursts of nonstop thirty-yard sprints, all under the watchful eye of Secretary of State Judy LaMarsh and other dignitaries.

The students were joined by some of Canada's best athletes: football quarterback Russ Jackson; national hockey team forward Fran Huck; Olympic bobsled gold medalist Vic Emery; weightlifter Pierre St-Jean; skier Nancy Greene; sprinter Harry Jerome; and runners Abby Hoffman, Marjorie Turner and Bill Crothers. Also in attendance was swimming sensation Elaine Tanner, the Mighty Mouse of the pool—who, at fifteen, was younger than some of the students.

Jerome, who had won an Olympic bronze in the 100-metre dash in 1964, recorded the best mark in the standing broad jump, with a leap of nine feet five inches. Not surprisingly, Jerome shared with Crothers, a middle-distance runner, the best time in the 300-yard run: forty-six seconds.

The sit-ups proved the toughest of the challenges. Jackson, the Ottawa Rough Riders quarterback and a rare professional at the event, managed just forty-six of them in one frantic minute: one short of a silver medal and six short of a gold. Jackson, Huck and St-Jean qualified only for bronze honours in the overall challenge, while Jerome, Tanner, Greene, Hoffman, Turner, speed skater Doreen McCannell and tennis player Bob Bedard met the gold standard.

Tanner completed sixty-seven sit-ups in sixty seconds, an effort nearly matched by fourteen-year-old schoolgirl Ginette Latulippe, who completed sixty-four in the showdown at the RA Centre sports facility, operated by the Recreation Association of the Public Service of Canada.

The demonstration was designed to draw attention to a fitness challenge that was to be completed by every primary and secondary student in Canada, including those attending schools for the disabled. Standards were established for every age group and badges were awarded in gold, silver and bronze. Those who failed to reach the standard received a red participatory badge. An estimated three and a half million boys and girls in twenty-four thousand schools took part in the test. About one million students earned a podium colour badge.

The badges were produced at a rate of thirty thousand per day by Montreal Swiss Embroidery Works Limited, in Ste-Thérèse, north of Montreal.

The standards were set after Ottawa schoolchildren had been tested. To attain a gold badge, a nine-year-old boy needed to jump at least five feet three inches; to perform at least forty-one sit-ups in one minute; to run 300 yards in sixty-six seconds; and to complete one of three optional tests: run 440 yards in ninety seconds; skate 184 yards in thirty-one seconds; or swim 50 yards in thirty-six seconds.

A sixteen-year-old girl was expected to jump at least six feet three inches in the standing broad jump; to complete thirty-nine sit-ups in one minute; and to run 300 yards in sixty-one seconds, before completing one of three optional standards. Schoolchildren were to choose between running 800 yards in three minutes and thirty seconds; skating 368 yards in fifty-two seconds; or swimming 100 yards in sixty-three seconds.

The fitness challenge, described by LaMarsh as the worthiest of all centennial initiatives, was inspired by a 1961 Ontario report about the woeful physical condition of children in the postwar era. The findings failed to generate any policy changes until centennial money flowed from federal coffers.

The centennial fitness program was soon succeeded by the Canada Fitness Award Program (and, later, by the Active Living Challenge Program), condemning generations of schoolchildren to huff and puff in front of their classmates. The fitness test became a cultural icon, referenced by the Tragically Hip in their "Fireworks" lyrics and featured in an episode of the television comedy *Corner Gas,* in which crotchety Oscar (Eric Peterson) called it Canada's last great achievement.

8

Expo 67

Centennial Centrepiece a Wild Success

A HALF-CENTURY LATER, EXPO 67 remains Canada's grandest performance on the world stage. Naysayers had predicted that the world's fair would be a disaster, a too-ambitious project sponsored by a megalomaniac mayor that required completion in too short a time. To the surprise of many, though not to its organizers, the 1967 International and Universal Exposition opened on time, on a spectacular site—two islands, one of them man-made, in the middle of the St. Lawrence River. Under the theme "Man and His World / *Terre des Hommes*," the fair avoided the trap of being a crass, commercial venture, instead presenting to the world a utopian vision in which innovation promised a future free of scarcity and filled with promise.

Millions Flock to World's Fair

They came under the river by Metro and they zipped over the river by Expo Express train. They came by automobile and they came by bus. They came by yacht (Queen Elizabeth ii, aboard *Britannia*) and they came by canoe (including voyageurs in the Centennial Canoe Pageant). They came by foot and they came by thumb, hitchhiking rides from strangers. They came as

A spectacular image at dusk of three popular pavilions on Île Notre-Dame (from left): Canada, Quebec and France. *Photo: Library and Archives Canada*

singles, in pairs, as families, and with church groups, service cubs, ethnic groups and sporting associations. And on they came, through sun and rain and transit strike. They came by the tens of thousands on the first day, and soon the counters registered in the millions. In the end, more than fifty million visitors were counted.

The first through the gates was a balding, thirty-nine-year-old jazz drummer from Chicago named Al Carter, whose schtick was to be the first—or the last, depending upon circumstances—to attend significant events. He claimed to be the first paying customer of the 1964 New York World's Fair and of the 1962 Seattle World's Fair. He also claimed to be the last person to mail a letter with a three-cent stamp and to be the final passenger carried by the last streetcar in Chicago. "I've been at some real swinging fairs before, but this has got to be the best one," he said. "I can just feel it. Man, it looks great."

The site was magnificent, an Oz in the middle of the St. Lawrence River. Even schoolchildren appreciated the pavilions' dramatic architecture: the geodesic dome of the United States pavilion, the sweeping roof of the Soviet Union exhibit, the tetrahedral-shaped Man the Explorer, West Germany's tent-like top, Britain's soaring tower, France's aluminum-ribbed hulk, and the inverted pyramid of Canada's showpiece. The Indians of Canada building looked like a giant teepee.

An elevated monorail snaked through the grounds, even piercing the American dome, giving riders a sneak peek at exhibits that others lined up

Two young women catch a nap while waiting for the gates of Expo 67 to open to the public on April 28. The first paying customer was Al Carter of Chicago, whose hobby it was to be the first—or, as the case may be, last—visitor of grand events. *Photo: Library and Archives Canada*

for hours to see. Alexander Calder's statue, *Man*, was a stainless-steel sentry. Moshe Safdie's pre-fab blocks stacked together at Habitat demonstrated that apartment blocks did not have to look like bricks.

In a city in which language was a contentious issue, Expo avoided disputes over word placement and letter size and grammar by using a series of

Moshe Safdie's Habitat '67 was constructed from prebuilt concrete blocks. The innovative housing project, built on an artificial peninsula jutting into the St. Lawrence River, did not revolutionize housing, as the architect had hoped, but it remains a landmark building popular with its residents. *Photo: Hubert Figuière / Flickr*

pictographs to guide visitors. A massive parking lot was divided into animal quadrants—moose, camel and hippo—so motorists and their young passengers could remember where the car was parked.

Telephone booths were open to the air, covered by mushroom caps of clear plastic. The street furniture was mundane in purpose—lights, benches, garbage cans, planters—but spectacular in execution, turning the exhibition grounds into the set for a futuristic science-fiction movie.

Even the name "Expo 67" seemed to belong to a language of its own, neither entirely English nor entirely French but identifiable to both—as optimistic of a future of mutual understanding, free of petty strife, as was Esperanto. In naming the fair, Mayor Jean Drapeau had taken a word from the title of a Maurice Chevalier song, "Le p'tite dame de l'Expo," which described a romance at a Paris exhibition before the war. The English-language media strongly objected, insisting upon using the title "Montreal World's Fair," until their stubborn stance began to look silly. The fair's success would convince the owners of the city's expansion team in major-league baseball to adopt the name "Expos" for the franchise.

One of the brilliant decisions in marketing Expo was the issuing of passports in lieu of admission tickets. The gold-embossed passports, with Julien Hébert's symbol and the fair's name rendered in lower-case Optima typeface as "expo67," looked so realistic that they came with a bilingual warning that they were not valid for entering a foreign country. A season pass included the holder's photograph and signature. Pages were left blank, to be rubber-stamped at the pavilions visited. Israel's stamp included a menorah, Australia's the familiar outline of the island nation. The passports remain a keepsake stored in attics across the country.

Just getting around the fair was an adventure, with many options: elevated, open-air Minirail; Expo Express; the Vaporetto motor launch; pedicab; hovercraft; or La Balade trailer train.

The crass commercialism of New York's recent world's fair was present here, too; the list of licensees in Expo's Official Guide included three pages of two columns each, running the gamut from ashtrays to flight bags to nail

BLOOD and RUM: THE CUBA PAVILION

Expo offered a taste of the forbidden, especially to Americans. The busy Cuba pavilion, which it was feared might be a target of anti-Castro bombers, showed bloody images of atrocities committed by the dictator Fulgencio Batista.

The pavilion had thirteen hostesses dressed in lightweight white wool dresses and white boots, whose job it was to extol the achievements of the revolution. Among these women was Dolores (Loly) Corona, a nineteen-year-old language student at the University of Havana. During the fair, she roomed with other Cubans in a spartan dormitory. Her one frustration consisted of her being accompanied by a Cuban chaperone every time she tried to explore Montreal on her own. She later became a prominent language educator in Cuba who worked with Canadian professors.

The Cuba pavilion sought to ease mistrust by selling rum drinks (a strategy also employed by the popular Jamaica pavilion, which sold a libation called the White Witch). Three Cuban singers and six musicians— playing guitars, trumpets, double bass and a conga drum—entertained the patrons waiting in line.

Among the many world leaders and celebrities feted at Expo 67 was Jacqueline Kennedy, the widowed First Lady whose arrival at the United States pavilion attracted hordes of well-wishers and the curious. *Photo: Library and Archives Canada*

DOGGONE DIGNITARIES

As the multitudes poured into Expo, so, too, did the famous and powerful. Among the dignitaries were Haile Selassie, the Emperor of Ethiopia, who brought his dog (a Chihuahua named Lulu); the Shah of Iran; Queen Juliana of the Netherlands; King Bhumibol Adulyadej and Queen Sirikit of Thailand; Princess Grace of Monaco; Jacqueline Kennedy; and French president Charles de Gaulle, who'd had the bad manners to shout "Vive le Québec libre!" from a balcony at Montreal City Hall. Stars of stage and screen also attended.

Senator Robert F. Kennedy, joined by his wife Ethel and seven children, attended Expo on July 5. After dutifully enduring some displays, the senator said, "I don't want my children to go through an education experience while they are here. I brought them to Expo to have fun." The family headed to La Ronde, where they enjoyed rides for two hours.

THE YEAR CANADIANS LOST THEIR MINDS AND FOUND THEIR COUNTRY

clippers. However, the kitsch seemed less prominent at Expo because this fair was far less interested in a hard sell. Most of the exhibitions were dedicated to examining humankind's journey, a history that provided a pathway to a future of limitless possibility—as long as we made the right decisions in an age of nuclear weapons and environmental despoliation. In the same afternoon, you could see a fragment of the Dead Sea Scrolls at the Israel pavilion and then talk on the futuristic Picturephone at the Telephone pavilion.

Expo was not immune from Cold War tensions. The American dome and the Soviet pavilion faced one another across the Le Moyne Channel separating Expo's two islands. Expo placed full-page advertisements in American magazines with a photo of the Soviet pavilion and the red hammer-and-sickle flag beneath the heading: "Look what the Russians are building, just 40 miles from the U.S.A. As an American, you should look into it."

Canada embarked on a changing sense of national identity through the celebrations with great changes still to come. The idea of one nation shared by two peoples would evolve into one of a nation of many peoples: one of them here from the beginning, and most of us arriving later from elsewhere. In 1967, Canadians invited the world and found their country's place in the world acknowledged. Those who attended Expo 67 would never forget it.

WINNING THE FAIR

This was supposed to have been Russia's show. In 1960, the International Bureau of Exhibitions, the Paris-based body that regulates world's fairs, narrowly voted in favour of Moscow as the host to a fair in 1967, the fiftieth anniversary of the Russian Revolution.

The Soviets backed out in April 1962—for fear, it has been said, that the abundance of household wonders to be displayed in the pavilions of decadent Western countries would create unrealistic consumer longings in Soviet citizens. The Soviets also argued that the upcoming world's fair planned for New York in 1964 and '65 would overshadow their own exposition.

Five months later, Montreal Mayor Jean Drapeau pitched his city as an alternative. The city won the right to stage a first-class fair, the first since the Brussels exhibition of 1958. The theme was to be "Man and His World / *Terre des Hommes*," adopted from French aviator-author Antoine de Saint-Exupéry's novel by that name. Instead of promoting a jingoistic nationalism or the superiority of one economic system over another, the fair was to present humankind at the centre of a changing world—one in which the future could be either marvellous or dystopian, depending upon man's decisions. An almost utopian vision would be presented.

L'Exposition universelle de 1967—
Le Spectacle du Siècle
The 1967 World Exhibition—
Show of the Century

expo67

28 AVRIL–27 OCTOBRE   APRIL 28–OCTOBER 27

MONTREAL CANADA

An aerial view of Île Notre-Dame, a man-made island in the middle of the St. Lawrence River. Today, it is also known as Parc Jean-Drapeau, named for the mayor many credited for the success of Expo 67. *Photo: Library and Archives Canada*

A promotional poster for Expo 67 promised the "show of the century." A savvy campaign lured many Americans north of the border to Montreal. *Photo: Library and Archives Canada*

Canada's striking inverted pyramid pavilion, named Katimivik, meaning "gathering place" in Inuktitut, the language of the Inuit people, was one of the more striking designs in an exposition filled with wonders. *Photo: Library and Archives Canada*

From the start, the Montreal fair had grand ambitions. It was to be half again as large as the one in Brussels in 1958 and about ten times the size of Seattle's world fair, Century 21 Exposition 1962, a Class B exhibition. Only later was the decision made to move the fair from the island of Montreal into the river surrounding it, by connecting two islands—Île Sainte-Hélène and the smaller Île Ronde—and building a new one, to be named Île Notre-Dame. Some of the landfill would come from excavations for the new subway system, due to open in 1966. (The decision to build a Metro line connecting central Montreal to the exhibition site and the South Shore meant scrapping another proposed line that was to have run north through a train tunnel beneath Mount Royal. That's how the city wound up with Metro lines numbered 1, 2, and 4.) Other dirt was to come from dredging the river bed; when even that was not enough, more lagoons were added to the plans.

Time was short. Not only had two years been lost as a result of the late bid, but a minority Progressive Conservative Government was replaced by a minority Liberal government. Drapeau, a practised politician, played the changes like a pro, knowing exactly who to prod and how to get approvals in the face of opposition. He failed to get a tower built on the Expo site—he had in mind something grander than even the Eiffel—but otherwise his scorecard was filled with successes.

The decision to create islands and a report issued by experts stating that the fair could not be completed by April 1967—that, in fact, it might not be ready to open its doors until 1969, or even 1970—led to the resignation of Expo's commissioner general and his team.

A new team was appointed. They would become known as *Les Durs*, the Tough Guys. There was Pierre Dupuy (commissioner general), a diplomat who would convince fifty-nine nations to participate; Robert Shaw (deputy commissioner), an engineer from Revelstoke, British Columbia, who kept his eye on the ticking countdown clock; Andrew Kniewasser (general manager); Colonel Edward Churchill (installations director); Pierre de Bellefeuille (exhibitions director); Yves Jasmin (publicity director); and Philippe de Gaspé Beaubien (operations director), better known as the Mayor of Expo.

The few years between Drapeau's bid and the fair's opening day had seen a rapid acceleration in Quebec's transformation from a rural, Church-based society to a dynamic culture elbowing its way onto the world stage. But Montreal, in 1967, was still a place where a francophone passenger refusing to show a train ticket to a unilingual anglophone conductor could be fined. Although Quebec was uninterested in celebrating Confederation during Centennial Year, Expo 67 offered the opportunity to express the aspirations of a people that for too long had felt denigrated and suppressed. Class and political tensions soon would find expression through violence and, not long afterward, through the ballot box. For now, in popular imagination, it was as if the Québécois had gone in one summer from being folkloric lumberjacks to global architects, engineers, and industrial designers and planners.

MUSIC, FILM, PROTEST AND PROBLEMS

The "sixties," as we now think of them, had not yet arrived. At Expo, women wore head scarves to keep their hair in place and many men wore suits and ties. Younger men sported hair that was more Beatle-length than Fabulous Furry Freak Brothers hirsute. But a spirit of change was afoot, and the place to find it was at the Youth pavilion at La Ronde.

In August, Jefferson Airplane and the Grateful Dead brought the Summer of Love vibe from San Francisco to a free La Ronde concert, whose highlight was a twenty-minute jam of "Gloria." Earlier in the summer, on June 1, Youth pavilion host Gilles Gougeon got his hands on a copy of the Beatles' latest album the day before it was to be released in North America. (A friend of a friend happened to be an Air Canada flight attendant returning that morning from London, where it had just been released.) Gougeon played the album over loudspeakers to the crowd gathered outside the pavilion for hour after hour, giving patrons the first public experience of *Sgt. Pepper's Lonely Hearts Club Band* in North America.

In another reflection of the times, eight men staged a silent anti-Vietnam War protest inside the United States pavilion on the fair's opening day. Officials gave them chairs and soft drinks and did not try to remove them.

A more bracing and eloquent protest was to be found at the Indians of Canada pavilion, fronted by a Kwakiutl totem pole of red cedar that had been carved by Tony and Henry Hunt of Alert Bay, British Columbia, on site during Expo. Exhibits depicted Aboriginal peoples in a pre-contact natural world and also highlighted the assistance that Indian guides had given to the explorers of Canada, including through the sharing of snowshoes and birchbark canoes. The wretched conditions experienced by contemporary First Nations, Inuit and Métis peoples were portrayed in photographs and in the distressing statistics about wealth and infant mortality. Hostesses informed visitors that Aboriginal children began their schooling by learning a foreign language. A sign near the exit demanded: "Give us the right to manage our own affairs." Canada had some historical reckoning to do during its year of celebration.

And Expo had problems of its own.

Huge crowds placed stress on all services, and lining up became de rigueur. Restaurants on site were expensive and food service could be slow. (A half-century later, St-Hubert BBQ still crows about how it avoided the problems that plagued others.) Bomb threats were made, and a pipe bomb was found and dismantled at Africa Place less than an hour before United Nations Secretary General U Thant was to tour the pavilion. A statue of the great Finnish runner Paavo Nurmi was damaged when vandals toppled it from its stand in front of Olympic House. The New York Urban League complained that, in filling 15,000 positions, Expo had hired only three black employees. Some politicians hinted that the Mafia was behind companies providing services at Expo. The Logexpo room-booking program was a fiasco that left many travellers stranded, or in substandard facilities. A fire destroyed many artefacts on display at Taiwan's museum. The Gyrotron ride at La Ronde broke down, trapping passengers.

A hostess for the Olympic pavilion at Expo 67 enjoys a brief respite on the lawn. The statue of the great Finnish runner Paavo Nurmi, in the background, was damaged by vandals late one night. *Photo: Library and Archives Canada*

In later years, guests could only hope they hadn't sat too close to the large green rock of asbestos ore set into a fountain at Asbestos Plaza at a time when its carcinogenic properties were not yet fully recognized.

Yet the failures and frustrations seemed slight in the face of the overwhelming experience that Expo provided. The architecture was fascinating, and so were the on-site sculptures. Live music played everywhere, with the steel bands on the water stage in front of the Trinidad and Tobago and Grenada pavilion proving to be particularly popular.

It was a time of innovation and experimentation in technology and the arts. The films shown at Expo 67 were diverse and remarkable, some seeking to immerse the viewer in a 360-degree experience, a harbinger of the digital age. (A 2014 volume of essays about film at Expo 67 would be appropriately titled *Reimagining Cinema*.) Christopher Chapman's *A Place to Stand*, commissioned by the government of Ontario for the province's pavilion, showed ninety minutes of film in a seventeen-minute running time by projecting several images simultaneously. It won an Academy Award for best live-action short subject, though it is remembered as much for its jaunty tune (by the husband-wife jingle-writing team of Dolores Claman and Richard Morris), whose title included the unforgettable "Ontar-i-ar-i-ar-i-o."

At the Labyrinth pavilion, viewers saw the Minotaur legend retold in three chambers, one with a cruciform screen and another with an L-shaped screen that projected images onto a wall and the floor, a precursor to the Imax technology that would thrill audiences in the coming years. At the Kaleidoscope pavilion, whose theme was colour and which was sponsored by six chemical companies, visitors were bathed in beams of coloured light in a mirrored chamber. The effect was described as the "ultimate psychedelic experience"—which indeed it must have been, at least for those who had yet to experience a drug-induced one.

THE ED SULLIVAN TREATMENT

Ed Sullivan took his millions of television followers on a visual tour of the world's fair site from the elevated vantage point of the monorail.

The American impresario broadcast two of his popular CBS Sunday evening entertainment spectacles from the Expo Theatre in May. The first featured the Supremes, an all-girl group, who performed "The Happening." The song was written by the Motown song-writing team of Holland-Dozier-Holland (Lamont Dozier and brothers Brian and Eddie Holland) for a comedy caper of the same name in which bored young drifters kidnap a Mafia kingpin. The movie was a stinker and a box-office bomb, but the up-tempo pop song climbed to the Billboard's No. 1 spot in the US a week after Diana Ross sang it before the cameras at Expo.

The Supremes appeared later in the May 7 episode, wearing 1920s flapper outfits, to sing a medley of "Thoroughly Modern Millie," "Second Hand Rose" and "Mame."

Other acts in the first episode included Spanish band leader Xavier Cugat with his singer protegé, María del Rosario Mercedes Pilar Martínez Molina Baeza, known by her stage name of Charo. The two had married the previous year, though the groom was more than four decades older than his bride. The bill was filled out by the coloratura soprano Roberta Peters ("Bell Song") and the Australian country singer Frank Ifield ("You Came Out of Nowhere" and "She Taught Me How to Yodel"). Other acts included the comedy duo of (Dick) Clair & (Jenna) McMahon, and Borscht Belt comic Corbett Monica, as well as the acrobatic Alcettys, a balancing act.

Among those introduced to the television audience during Sullivan's trademark "audience bow" was Montreal mayor Jean Drapeau, whose first name the host produced as "Gene."

THE YEAR CANADIANS LOST THEIR MINDS AND FOUND THEIR COUNTRY

The second show, which aired on May 21, included local content, as thirty-two-year-old, Montreal-born pianist Ronald Turini played with accompaniment from the Montreal Symphony Orchestra. The orchestra also performed with dramatic soprano Birgit Nilsson of the Royal Swedish Opera, who sang "In questa reggia," an aria from the Puccini opera *Turandot*.

The *chansonnier* Claude Léveillée, who three years earlier had become the first Québécois artist to perform solo at Montreal's Place des Arts, sang "Le rendez-vous," a signature tune that he had released on an eponymous album for Columbia Records six years earlier.

Pop acts included Australia's The Seekers singing "Georgy Girl" and Petula Clark performing "Don't Sleep in the Subway," which she'd released the previous month. She also sang "This is My Song" and a medley, including her huge hit, "Downtown."

The comic Alan King did a stand-up routine, while Expo provided a backdrop as dancers choreographed by Peter Gennaro danced in front of various pavilions. Traditional Quebec square dancing and clog dancing were performed by the ensemble known as Les Feux Follets.

Drapeau was introduced again from the audience, as was Pierre Dupuy, the commissioner general of the world's fair.

GETTING TO EXPO

The roads to Montreal were busy. Trains and buses were crammed. Airplanes landed at Dorval International Airport with no empty seats.

Some visitors found more unconventional transit.

Model T

Like many, Jack Lillico drove to Expo. Unlike them, he did so at the wheel of a 1926 Model T Ford Depot Hack. Setting out from the West Coast, the Vancouver magician led a convoy of vintage automobiles, many of them restored jalopies. His Model T carried a sign over the front windscreen reading, "Across Canada Centennial Tour." They hit patches of high water going through Rogers Pass in the Rockies. The Model T made it through the high water without problem, though the escorting RCMP vehicle needed repairs in the next town. Here's something to think about: Lillico's Model T was as old in 1967 as a 1976 model would be in 2017.

OPPOSITE: Jack Lillico motors his 1926 Model T Ford Depot Hack down a ramp at Toronto's futuristic City Hall. The magician drove his jalopy from Vancouver to Montreal to attend Expo 67. *Photo: Doug Griffin / Toronto Star*

Roller Skates

Christopher Robin Price quit his job as a cook in Vancouver, strapped on a pair of roller skates at the entrance gates to the University of British Columbia, and headed east. The twenty-year-old wanted to see Expo, to get to Montreal as cheaply as possible, and to do so in a way that no one else was doing. "When I first left Vancouver, motorists used to laugh when they passed me," he said. "Now they stop and give me money for meals." He cadged beds and food along the way, occasionally spending a night in jail or a firehouse. He was armed with a starter's gun to scare off predatory wildlife.

Foot

The famed Australian distance runner Bill Emmerton ran from Toronto City Hall to Expo's Australia pavilion, though he faltered on the final leg—his pacing put off by a policeman's mistaken assertion that he was near his goal. He arrived at last desperately thirsty, near tears and exhausted. The Tasmanian legend, who twice attempted to run the length of Britain from John O'Groats in Scotland to Land's End in England, was joined for the final hundred metres by his wife, Norma, a Canadian. Having endured his Toronto-to-Montreal run in sapping humidity, the following year he decided to conquer one of the most inhospitable stretches of the continent, leading to the memorable headline in the *Los Angeles Herald Examiner,* "Man Believed Sane Runs Through Death Valley."

Canoes

Not one but dozens of canoeists headed for Expo.

On April 1—a day, it should be noted, for fools—four men eased their canoe into the mighty Fraser River at New Westminster, British Columbia. They began paddling upstream through ice-choked rivers and snowy mountain passes. Conditions often were poor, circumstances often hazardous. They needed five days to portage by ski through Howe Pass in the Rockies.

The canoeists—Ralph Brine, Don McNaughton, Dr. David Chisholm and Jim Reid—at last arrived at Expo 67 on July 15, the journey speeded up by occasional use of an outboard motor. They brought with them a pair of cufflinks from the Royal City, as New Westminster is known (a gift for Montreal Mayor Jean Drapeau), as well as two thousand pieces of mail to be posted from Expo. They returned home with an engraved silver tray to be presented to New Westminster's mayor. Brine later wrote a book called *Canada's Forgotten Highway: A Wilderness Canoe Route from Sea to Sea.*

"At one time we were in real danger on the North Saskatchewan River as we hauled our canoe over the ice," Brine, a shoe-store owner, said at the time. "It would have been very easy to fall into the water and drown. Another time, later on, we had to bivouac for a week while ice melted on one of the rivers we were travelling on."

The New Westminster quartet had sponsors to cover their costs. A bank loan financed another epic canoe odyssey, undertaken by two young men compelled by a spirit of adventure.

Twenty-year-old Geoff Davis and twenty-two-year-old Ken McRae were taking pre-law studies at the University of Victoria when they decided to put aside books for a year to celebrate the Centennial. On June 24, they splashed their cedar canoe into the Peace River at Taylor, British Columbia, and

POLAR
ambassadors

Early in the year, bush pilot Ray Munro and geophysicist Ivan Christopher left Montreal on a twenty-six-day goodwill tour of the High Arctic and remote northern communities, as polar ambassadors on behalf of Expo 67.

Munro's biography was as unlikely as it was incredible. The clipping library at the *Montreal Gazette* included three separate files for a Ray Munro—one for a polar ambassador, one for a mining executive and one for a muckraking tabloid editor. All were the same man.

Born in Montreal, he had learned to fly as a teenager and soon enough was piloting Spitfires during the war. After being wounded in action, he worked as a bush pilot and a photojournalist. His investigation into corruption in the Vancouver police department led to two suicides and the police chief's quitting in disgrace. Bored by life as a muckraking journalist, Munro became a balloonist and a distinguished parachutist. He was the first to pilot a balloon across the Irish Sea, earning an entry in the *Guinness Book of Records* for parachute jumping closest to the North Pole—an undertaking in which he suffered serious injuries.

In between adventures, he befriended such Hollywood stars as Marilyn Monroe and Errol Flynn while serving as their private pilot. He also toured Canada as a hypnotist, billed as "The Great Raymond."

To a swashbuckler like Munro, a 14,000-kilometre tour of Yellowknife, Inuvik, Tuktoyaktuk, Dawson City and Watson Lake in a Cessna 180 that lacked instruments was virtually a vacation.

The massive France pavilion, designed by architects Jean Faugeron and André Blouin, rose nine stories above the exhibition grounds, showing off a striking outer aluminum skeleton. The building remains one of few from Expo 67 to survive, now home to a casino and entertainment complex. *Photo: Library and Archives Canada*

headed east, retracing Alexander Mackenzie's route in the reverse direction. The young men were armed with topographical maps and knowledge gleaned from reading histories of the coureurs des bois.

"The route we took was an old fur-trading route, so there were lots of natural places to stop," Davis told *Vancouver Sun* journalist Frances Bula, on the fortieth anniversary of his journey. More than once, they spilled into the water, nearly losing the canoe. "At the headwaters of the Churchill, we were paddling along and we didn't hear the noise [of rushing water]. We went into a chute that ended in standing waves at the bottom."

They arrived in Winnipeg in late July, taking in some action at the Pan

American Games, before resuming their journey. They arrived in Ottawa on October 1, landing on the banks of the Ottawa River directly below the Parliament Buildings. They carried with them a letter of greeting from the BC lieutenant governor, to be given to the governor general. Of course, the vice-regal representative is not usually found in the Parliamentary precincts, so the young men were taken instead to meet the prime minister. "I used to do some canoeing," Lester Pearson told them.

When they docked in Montreal, they were given free passes to Expo in honour of their brave, if foolhardy, adventure. (For a fortnight on the isolated Churchill River in Saskatchewan, the pair had run perilously low on provisions.)

A little later, another team of canoeists with a similar route arrived at Expo.

Ice was still on the banks of the Peace River when Adolf Ikert and crew first slipped their canoe into the high, frigid waters. The boat would be their workplace for the next three months.

Ikert had been planning for years a transcontinental trip that would follow—though in reverse—the route taken by Alexander Mackenzie to the Pacific. His crew included a farmer, a radiographer, two students and two trappers, including René Frigon, a French Canadian and a local legend known as the Tarzan of the North, who brought along his three-year-old wolf-German shepherd cross, Lobo.

A Polish-born immigrant who owned a variety and lumber store in Pouce Coupe, British Columbia, Ikert was fascinated with the history of his adopted land and wanted to pay homage to the explorers during Centennial Year. His canoe was named the "Mackenzie Explorer." The new Canadian flag was painted on its bow, the centennial symbol on the hull.

An advance crew included a realtor, a barkeep and another trapper. They would stop in hamlets and towns along the route, to ballyhoo the pending

Rose Parade Envoys

The schemes to promote Expo 67 and other centennial celebrations south of the border included the clever placement of a float representing Canada in the nationally televised Tournament of Roses parade in Pasadena, California. The four young women sent as ambassadors were Miss Canada Barbara Lynne Kelly and Expo hostesses Marilyn Young, Michele St-Amant and Martha Labelle Daly. The *Los Angeles Times* greeted them with the headline: "Chilled Canadian Beauties Warm Up to Rose Parade Task."

visit and to sell souvenirs to finance the journey. The paddlers stroked shirtless when conditions permitted, but donned costumes—furs, moose hides and mukluks—when there was an audience. Ikert, who grew a long, unkempt beard during the odyssey, wore a fringed, sleeveless buckskin shirt and a tricorne hat. He waved a cutlass for photographers.

The crew arrived in Detroit in early August, looking like movie extras dropped into the big city. They were regarded as savages from the wilderness. "Everyone carries his load here," crew member Bill Frost, a farmer, told the *Detroit Free Press*. "Even Lobo carries a pack on portage." Their reward in the big city was a complimentary night's stay at the swanky Pontchartrain Hotel.

A month later, they paddled to Île Sainte-Hélène at Expo 67, where they were met by marina Vice-Commodore Les Crout. They had left Pouce Coupe on May 13, and arrived in Montreal on August 31.

After the Fair

Expo was still in full swing as debate raged about what to do after its closing. Some suggested a permanent fair. Others wanted the islands to be transferred to the United Nations. The follow-up exhibition, known as Man and His World, would continue to issue passports, running as a summer festival until 1984.

The US pavilion caught fire in 1976 and remained a ruin for nearly two decades before reopening as the Biosphere, a museum dedicated to the environment. The France and Quebec pavilions were converted into casino complexes. Much of the rest was razed or was left to rot *in situ*.

The decaying pavilions on Île Notre-Dame, which retained their futuristic look from certain angles, appeared as a ruined alien city in a 1979 episode, entitled "Greetings from Earth," of the science-fiction TV series *Battlestar Galactica*. Notre Dame eventually would become the site of a motorsport park and car-racing circuit. Habitat was preserved and was used as a permanent residence. Dedicated fans gathered on the internet to discuss the state of disrepair of other buildings. After South Korea's pavilion had seen service as a Man and His World exhibit for Canada Post and the Royal Canadian Mint, its neglected tower and roof continued to stand.

—

SOME OF EXPO'S buildings were moved and repurposed. The Soviets disassembled their pavilion and sent it to Moscow, to become a component of the

Exhibition of Economic Achievements. The structure itself is known to locals as the "Montreal Building."

The Jeunesses Musicales du Canada/Young Canada Music pavilion was moved east, to Mont Orford in Quebec's Eastern Townships, where it still is used as part of the Orford Music Academy. The Yugoslavia pavilion was purchased for one hundred dollars, then dismantled and shipped to Newfoundland, where it is now the Southern Newfoundland Seamen's Museum in the town of Grand Bank. A dory, the boat from which generations of Newfoundlanders worked the Grand Banks' underwater plateaus, rests in the lobby of the building, whose triangular roofline is said to resemble the sails of a schooner.

The Czechoslovakia pavilion also was relocated to Newfoundland. It was a gift from a nation in mourning, in recognition of the good deeds of strangers. On September 5, 1967, a Czechoslovakia State Airlines turbo-prop crashed soon after takeoff at Gander. Thirty-two passengers were killed on impact and five others died later in hospital. Another thirty-two survived the crash, most of whom were saved by the quick response of rescue and hospital workers—including a helicopter pilot who flew burn victims to treatment centres. The restaurants and the small theatre in the original building sent by the grateful Czechoslovakians were reassembled in Gander. The pavilion's larger exhibition area was rebuilt in Grand Falls, where it is now known as the Gordon Pinsent Centre for the Arts.

———

AN ACCOUNT OF what had been experienced that magic summer was offered by Toronto critic Robert Fulford in his 1968 book, *This Was Expo*. As he observed:

> *Man, in his mind and imagination, has moved beyond scarcity. Man now has the knowledge to make a world of material comfort for every human creature on earth. We, the collective creators of our own world, can now feed everyone, can now house everyone, can now build modern cities of great beauty and high efficiency, can now distribute art and information to everyone.*
>
> *Science and technology have made all things possible; but they remain, for now, only possibilities. Between the idea and the reality there still stands an army of problems—dead orthodoxies of nationalism and bureaucracy, of stunted imaginations and timid minds. Expo's function was to indicate the material and spiritual resources of the world of men, make them coherent,*

Julien Hébert's circular symbol of stick figures with raised arms was criticized by Parliament, but the Expo 67 symbol became as recognizable as the maple leaf. *Photo: Library and Archives Canada*

and show how we can use them if we have the courage to do so.

Controversy Over Symbol and Song

BOLD DESIGN BAFFLES MPS

The December afternoon grew long as the House of Commons tidied up business in preparation for the 1963 Christmas break. Before carols were sung to express yuletide joy, the House sat for the second reading of Bill C-120, an act to amend the Canadian World Exhibition Corporation Act. What seemed a dreary bit of procedural housecleaning soon devolved into a free-for-all of art criticism.

The House members did not care for the graphic symbol that had been approved by the directors of the world's fair and presented to Prime Minister Lester Pearson two months earlier.

The Leader of the Opposition was first to weigh in. "I must say it is difficult to understand," confessed John Diefenbaker. "It is a series of angles facing one another in a regular arrangement around a circle."

It fell to Minister of Public Works Jean-Paul Deschatelets to defend the logo. "The design was conceived by an artist, Mr. [Julien] Hébert, who had the idea of joining two symbolic figures of man to convey the idea of friendship and fraternity. By a clever grouping in the form of a circle of eight of these double figures, the artist suggested the form of the earth, that is the world of men, without resorting to the usual graphic interpretation which can be seen on any truck passing in the street."

Diefenbaker was having none of it, employing the my-child-can-draw-better method of art criticism. "When I was a boy, we used to draw men like that: just two or three lines," he told the Commons. "It was simple. It was the only artistry we could indulge in. To me, this looks like an artistic monstrosity. I would have thought that this would be an ideal occasion to place the maple leaf

Expo 67 took pride in not being as commercial an exhibition as the recent New York World's Fair, but there was no shortage of souvenirs to be purchased, including mugs, ashtrays, lighters, flight bags and round suitcases. *Photo: Library and Archives Canada*

in the centre, to show it was Canadian." (Diefenbaker would object, months later, to a proposed Canadian flag with a maple leaf in the centre.)

A Progressive Conservative backbencher opined that the proposed world's fair logo resembled the peace symbol used by groups seeking nuclear disarmament.

Reid Scott, an NDP member from Toronto, dismissed the graphic as a "weird-looking thing."

A Social Credit lumberman from the Cariboo, British Columbia, said that the symbol "looks like a combination of a tractor wheel and a bunch of power poles."

A Ralliement des Créditistes member from Quebec complained that the design had no bilingual character.

Inspired, Diefenbaker again was on his feet. "I have never seen a monstrosity like it. It will bring ridicule to Canada."

A Liberal from Ontario, a former journalist, insisted that he saw in the design the letters "M" and "W," likely standing for "Montreal" and "World's fair," which to him was unacceptable; the fair belonged to Canada rather than to any one city, while the "W" for "World" did not reflect the word's French equivalent.

Minister Deschatelets assured the member that the letter "M" thing had been looked at and dismissed; it was incidental to the design.

A Conservative suggested that flying pigeons be added to the design.

Another Conservative, coincidentally named Pigeon (Louis-Joseph, from Point-aux-Trembles, Quebec), insisted upon the addition of a maple leaf to the design.

Walter Dinsdale, a Conservative social worker from Manitoba, repeated the suggestion of a maple leaf. This sentiment was supported by BC New Democrat Bert Herridge, a forest farmer from the Kootenays, who confessed that he was neither a post-impressionist nor a cubist, so did not understand the design.

Gerald Reagan, a Liberal lawyer from Halifax, dismissed the logo as a "beatnik type of symbol," thus forging all-party agreement on the artistic merit of the design.

Liberal Secretary of State Jack Pickersgill was not impressed by the tenor of the debate. "May I say that the argument we have had for the last few minutes illustrates why legislative bodies never legislate art," he said, before adding, "We are not elected to parliament in our capacity as art critics, but for other reasons."

The world's fair board had considered several submissions before settling on Hébert's simple, elegant design. Its component figures, based upon an ancient graphic symbol of a man—a vertical line with diagonally outstretched arms—were joined into pairs to represent fellowship. Eight of these pairs were arranged to form a circle, a clever representation of the earth. As an emblem, it emphasized humanity's place in the world.

In devising the symbol, Hébert said he was reminded of a poem entitled "La ronde autour de monde," by the French Symbolist Paul Fort. The poem imagined the circle that would be created if everyone in the world were to hold hands.

———

THE BOARD APPROVED the design in a meeting at the fair site on Île Sainte-Hélène in August. In October, Commissioner General Pierre Dupuy unveiled the design to the public, before making a presentation of a sign with the symbol to the prime minister in the Centre Block in Ottawa.

The displeasure expressed by the members of Parliament in December led a world's fair spokesman to say that the board would reconsider the submissions.

THE TALENTED DESIGNER

Julien Hébert, designer of the Expo 67 symbol, was born in Rigaud, Quebec, a town on the Ottawa River whose shrine, Our Lady of Lourdes, attracted many pilgrims. He entered the École des Beaux-Arts in Montreal at the age of nineteen, later studying at the Université de Montréal.

"I became a designer, because I studied both sculpture and philosophy," he said years later, as quoted by Martin Racine for the website CanadianDesignResource.ca. "Sculpture is related to the form, the sensual, the touch. Philosophy is the mind, the reflection. Moving to design was a logical step."

After an apprenticeship in Paris with the Russian-born sculptor Ossip Zadkine, Hébert returned to Montreal at a time when artists were beginning to confront the Church and state in Quebec, notably through a manifesto known as "Le Refus global" ("Total Refusal"). His contribution to the changing tide would be an insistence that Canada design and produce its own goods, rather than merely export raw materials while importing finished products from others.

In 1951, Hébert won the first design competition in Canada, launched by the federal trade and commerce ministry to promote the conversion of wartime industries for peacetime use. His winning entry, a chaise lounge made of bent tubular forms set on a triangular base, was displayed at the Milan Triennial in 1954 and was added to the Museum of Modern Art's collection in New York. Additionally, it was featured in such publications as *Domus*. He was hired by a Canadian steel and aluminum manufacturer to design furniture.

Hébert was a founding member of the Canadian Association of Industrial Designers, and later served as president of the group. In 1963, the Quebec government awarded him four thousand dollars in an artistic competition for his design of a school desk. He went on to design the Quebec and Canada pavilions for Expo 70, in Osaka, Japan. Hébert's credits also include postage stamps and other logos, as well as a wall at the Salle Wilfrid-Pelletier in Place des Arts in Montreal, a mural in the Montreal Metro station at Saint-Henri, and the roof of the Opera Hall in the National Arts Centre in Ottawa.

Julien Hébert, who created the Expo 67 symbol, was a brilliant industrial designer who believed Quebecers and Canadians should design their own products. He won a postwar contest designed to encourage the transformation of wartime factories for the production of consumer goods with a simple, magnificent chair made from aluminum tubing. *Photo: Michel Brault*

Hébert was asked if he would conjure another symbol. "Not for the House of Commons," he replied.

The *Ottawa Journal*'s editorial board agreed with the parliamentarians that the design was uninspired, a result of "lazy designing, more mechanical than creative." At the same time, the newspaper felt the designer should be leery about the aesthetic judgments of politicians. The paper helpfully suggested the world's fair encourage some "Eskimo artists" to submit designs.

Less than three months later, the fair's board of directors quietly issued a statement announcing that the symbol would be retained. The board bemoaned the fact that there had been no emblem since the parliamentary critique, noting, "Moreover, it appears far from certain that any new emblem would receive unanimous approval." The MPS' instruction to find a better design by the end of 1964 was ignored.

The dispute over his symbol for the world's fair (created before the name "Expo 67" had been determined) unsettled Hébert. His design, confirmed by the board, was bold and uncomplicated, evoking an impression of hands lifted in celebration or worship.

The symbol won prizes for its success as a trademark, while commercial licensing earned more than $500,000 in the year before the fair opened its doors.

Hébert's symbol appeared on Canada's commemorative five-cent stamp for Expo 67, which featured Canada's inverted pavilion, known as Katimivik (Inuktitut for "gathering place"). He also coordinated the design of part of the pavilion's interior.

The symbol that politicians had so denigrated captured the spirit of Expo: universal, fraternal, optimistic and exuberant. Those who saw it then immediately recognize it now.

"HEY FRIEND" FINDS FEW

The world's fair needed a theme song. "I'm looking for a second 'Meet Me in St. Louis,'" said the fair's head of popular entertainment. "I want something that is easily whistleable on first hearing."

Less than a year before Expo's gates were to open, a song-writing contest was announced by Le Festival du Disque, backed by the world's fair corporation and sponsored by the Sun Life Assurance Company. The contest was open to residents of any country participating in Expo. The rules stipulated that the song needed to be written in a universally popular style, with lyrics in either English or French. Budding tunesmiths had three months to complete their works.

The prize consisted of five thousand dollars in cash, future royalties from worldwide rights, and a premiere at the second annual Festival du Disque in

The elegant actress and singer Renée Claude joined singer Gilles Vigneault and song-writer Stéphane Venne at Expo 67. Venne wrote "Un jour, un jour" ("Hey Friend, Say Friend" in the English version), the official song for the world's fair. *Photo: Library and Archives Canada.*

Montreal, in October 1966, followed by a performance at the gala opening of the fair the following April.

The entries poured in. Some 2,210 songs arrived, from thirty-five nations. These were culled to thirty songs, which then were deliberated upon by a three-person jury, comprising a French *parolier* (composer), an English lyricist and a third musician. The trio, whose identities were never revealed, resigned after being unable to determine a winner.

Their stalemate was not because of a dispute over preferred songs. Rather, they found none of the submissions to be of sufficient merit. An appealing entry from a Czech composer had to be rejected because it was scored for a symphony orchestra.

A second jury, consisting of three Expo representatives and one each from the festival and the sponsor, settled upon "Un jour, un jour" ("Hey Friend, Say Friend" in English) by twenty-five-year-old Quebec composer Stéphane Venne. He'd already released two albums, both of them eponymous and marked "Vol. 1" and "Vol. 2," and had some fifty of his one hundred and fifty compositions recorded.

The handsome, square-jawed, brooding composer said he was making more of an artistic statement than seeking a pop hit. "I didn't want it to be commercial," he said. "I wanted it poetical." The self-taught musician was inspired by a spread in a French-language newspaper showing an artistic rendition of the fairgrounds. He apparently entered his hand-written score just minutes before the deadline, having learned of the contest when the songwriters' guild sent him an entry form.

The theme song debuted on an hour-long CBC television special that fall, sung in both English and French. The English lyrics were by Marcel Stellman.

A number of recordings were rushed to market, to cash in on what many labels were certain would be a money-maker, given the massive interest in Expo. The first release likely was RCA Victor's instrumental 45 RPM in both march and rumba-beguine tempos by organist Lucien Hétu, later appointed the official *carillonneur* (bell player) of Expo 67. The London label released a rollicking country-and-western rendition by Marcel Martel, a well-known singing cowpoke from Drummondville, Quebec.

Venne's own single was issued on the Select label with an orchestra conducted by Marcel Lévesque, a recording remarkable for the singer's exaggerated consonant rolling and the orchestra's honking horns. The flip side was "Ces

DOLPHINS GET IT RIGHT

A remarkable version of "Hey Friend, Say Friend" that went unrecorded was performed by four dolphins under the guidance of trainer Al Panagakos at the Expo aquarium in May. As an organ played the theme, the dolphins popped their heads out of the water to whistle and click through the chorus of the song, delighting their audience, including Robert Shaw, Expo's deputy commissioner general.

THE YEAR CANADIANS LOST THEIR MINDS AND FOUND THEIR COUNTRY

temps de jeunesse." The composer was shown on the jacket posed before a giant Expo logo carved into concrete at Place des Nations, a cigarette pinched between two fingers.

The tune was criticized for its European "yé-yé" beat, a bubblegum-pop style of music trending at the time in France and the Iberian countries, though Venne insisted he had more of a jazzy beat in mind.

A week after its release, a reporter from the *Gazette* in Montreal contacted disc jockeys across the United States to see if the song was generating interest in the upcoming Expo. A spot check from Boston to Los Angeles failed to find a single radio deejay familiar with the song.

Worse, some stations that played the song vowed never to do so again. At CKNL in Fort St. John, British Columbia, the program director played the English vocal and an instrumental version of the theme song only once each, before announcing that it would air no more. "It is our way of saying it is lousy music," Bob Loeppky said. "About two dozen people called to say it was lousy. Only two said it was great, including a twelve-year-old listener."

He criticized the song for not citing Expo 67 or even the city of Montreal, neither of which appear in the lyrics. A similar complaint was attributed to Montreal mayor Jean Drapeau. However, Venne ably defended his song in an interview on CBC Radio.

In her own recording of the song on the Trans-Canada label, Michèle Richard addressed the supposed problem with a tuneful chant that mentioned Expo before getting to the lyrics.

Perhaps the most successful version was a zippy single on the Jupiter label by Donald Lautrec, a one-time bodyguard whose own singing career grew during the mid-1960s. By mid-summer, his version had sold seventy thousand copies. It also was released in France and England.

With English versions widely panned as cloying, resistance to the song remained steadfast. "Expo 67 has announced that its theme song, 'Hey Friend, Say Friend' will be played daily at the fair on the world's largest carillon," one newspaper editorialized. "Is that an announcement or a threat?"

In any case, the official Expo 67 song was outshone by Bobby Gimby's ubiquitous "Canada."

9 Ongoing Reminders

From Self-Government to a UFO Pad

CENTENNIAL SCHOOLS AND centennial parks can now be found across the land. Museums and libraries were built, as each provincial and territorial capital undertook a major construction project designed to improve the cultural life of the nation. Remnants of Expo 67, which had not been intended as a permanent exhibition, live on: the former US pavilion serves as the Biosphere ecological museum, the French and Quebec pavilions serve as casino complexes, and La Ronde remains an amusement park. You'll come across the centennial symbol in the most unexpected places—in a waterfront park in Kingston, Ontario; at the Centennial Monument at Westmount Park in Montreal; or atop the Rosehill Reservoir in Toronto. The Centennial left a physical legacy.

Self-Rule, Flag in North

After decades of rule from far-off Ottawa, the Northwest Territories acquired a home government in 1967. The federal government selected the mining town of Yellowknife as the territorial capital—bitterly disappointing residents of the rival mining town of Fort Smith, the administrative centre for the territories.

The Yukon Territory joined Confederation during the 1898 gold rush, then went sixty-nine years without an official flag. The Royal Canadian Legion launched a contest as a centennial project. On December 1, the territorial government adopted a design submitted by Lynn Lambert of Destruction Bay. The Yukon coat of arms is displayed on the centre panel framed by two stems of fireweed. The tricolour panels represent the forests (green), snow (white), and lakes and rivers (blue). *Photo: Open Clip Art Library*

On September 18, two chartered D7 propeller planes—one loaded with bureaucrats (and a civil servant's pet skunk), the other with papers and office furniture—landed in Yellowknife from Ottawa, for the official handover of power. Upon arrival, the first resident commissioner proclaimed, "At last, we are home!" Stuart Hodgson, a war veteran and long-time labour organizer, had helped to establish the territorial government in scattered offices located in a school, a curling rink and a bowling alley. When asked by the prime minister to serve as commissioner, Hodgson had protested, "But I don't know that much about government." Pearson replied, "That's why I'm sending you."

During his time as commissioner, Hodgson would earn the nickname *"Umingmak"* ("Muskox").

A hundred and one years earlier, the Yukon territory had been carved from the vast northern territories. Nunavut was established as a separate territory in 1999.

The land of the midnight sun, where prospectors sought fortunes in the detritus of glacial river beds, lacked a flag to fly over the Klondike. As a centennial project, the Whitehorse branch of the Royal Canadian Legion sought to remedy this by holding a contest.

A hundred and thirty-seven submissions came in from aspiring flag designers. Ten of the proposals were the work of Lynn Lambert of Destruction Bay, a recent graduate of the drafting program of the Yukon Vocation and Training Centre (now Yukon College). One of his designs was declared the victor, after which it was amended slightly to satisfy heraldic standards. He received a hundred dollars for his efforts.

Lambert's winning entry displayed three vertical panels: green on the inner edge, representing forests; blue on the outer edge, symbolizing Yukon's rivers and lakes; and a larger central panel of white, for snow—of which the territory

A fading way of life on Cape Breton Island is commemorated at the Miner's Museum, a centennial project backed by Nina Cohen, who also instigated the Men of the Deeps choir. *Photo: Ron A. Sheyan*

has no shortage. Yukon's distinctive crest, which incorporates gold disks and is topped by a Malamute sled dog, appears in the central panel above two branches of fireweed (*Epilobium angustifolium*), the territory's floral emblem.

The Council of the Yukon Territory adopted the flag on December 1, 1967.

Miners' Tribute Museum

Though wealthy and a stranger to life in the mines or life as the wife of a miner, Nina Cohen believed in recording and preserving the hardscrabble existence of those who extracted wealth from the unforgiving rock of Cape Breton Island. As the coal industry declined through the twentieth century, it became clear that such a way of life would be forever altered. With government money available as the Centennial approached, Cohen—from Glace Bay, Cape Breton—led the campaign to raise money to build a museum.

The community's share came to more than $150,000, a substantial sum for a region struggling with an economic restructuring. Cohen, who at the time was national president of Hadassah-WIZO, a philanthropic association of Jewish women, became a tireless advocate on behalf of the project, organizing meetings in which the contents and architecture of the museum were discussed, as well as raising funds. A $10,000 donation from the United Mine Workers helped prime the pump.

The philanthropist Nina Cohen was the moving force behind the creation of the Cape Breton Miners' Museum in Glace Bay. Her determination in finding funding for the project earned her the honour of unveiling the cornerstone on July 31, 1967. *Photo: Cape Breton Miners' Museum*

Her intent was to create a place where mineworkers would not be ignored in the telling of history. She believed the stories of mine families were an important part of the Canadian mosaic, one too often ignored. The attraction would lure tourists to the island, creating an economy to replace the one disappearing with coal's decline.

When the museum opened on July 31, 1967, Cohen unveiled the cornerstone in the presence of the lieutenant-governor, the provincial attorney general, a federal cabinet minister, Secretary of State Judy LaMarsh and Premier Robert Stanfield—who was taking a break from his campaign for the national leadership of the Progressive Conservative party.

Cross-Canada Building Spree

The Confederation Memorial Program offered $2.5 million to each province and territory to build cultural centres in the capitals to mark the Centennial.

men OF THE DEEPS

The members of the Men of the Deeps choir were working or retired coal miners from Nova Scotia's Cape Breton island. Their songs, conveying the folklore of those whose lives revolved around a collapsing industry, were presented to audiences at Expo 67. Jack O'Donnell, a university professor who collected coal-mining songs, was the choral group's founding director. Folklorist Helen Creighton assisted in the gathering of traditional songs for performance. Notices seeking singers for a choir associated with the new miners' museum were posted in men's wash houses.

With several recordings now to its credit, the choir is known for its dramatic entrance at concerts—the men marching out of the black of a darkened hall, their way lit by the bobbing lights on their miners' helmets. The Men of the Deeps became the first Canadian performers to tour the People's Republic of China after diplomatic relations were restored. The coal miners' chorus currently has a rehearsal space at the Cape Breton Miners' Museum in Glace Bay.

The Men of the Deeps, formed of working coal miners from Cape Breton, performed at Expo 67. The choir, still active, is known for its dramatic entrance in the dark, their way lit by the beam of light from their helmets. *Photo: Cape Breton Miners' Museum*

Two Maritime provinces—Nova Scotia and New Brunswick—used the money to complete utilitarian projects not of a cultural nature, a crass squandering of opportunity. Saskatchewan split its allotted funds to build arts centres in its two largest cities.

Here's how the provinces spent their money:

Newfoundland: *Arts and Cultural Centre (St. John's)*

The centre opened on May 22, 1967. It features a nine-hundred-seat proscenium theatre, a seventy-five-seat basement theatre, libraries, art galleries and catering services.

Nova Scotia: *Tupper Building (Halifax)*

The Tupper Building is a fifteen-storey high-rise with a two-storey annex. It became the new home of Dalhousie University's medical school. It was named after Sir Charles Tupper, a diplomat and physician who was a Father of Confederation and who served as a premier, a prime minister (for ten weeks in 1896, the shortest tenure ever), and founding president of the Canadian Medical Association.

New Brunswick: *Centennial Building (Fredericton)*

Occupying a prominent half-block in downtown Fredericton, the Centennial Building opened on March 14, 1967, the first of the projects to be completed under the Centennial Memorial program. The six-storey modernist structure has a T-shaped plan and houses more than one thousand provincial employees. Each floor includes a mural depicting a theme from New Brunswick's history or industry.

Quebec: *Grand Théâtre de Québec (Quebec City)*

Two concert halls are the grandest features of a building that was not completed until 1971. The Shamrock Summit, between Prime Minister Brain Mulroney and U.S. President Ronald Reagan, was held at this complex in 1985.

Ontario: *Centennial Centre of Science and Technology (Toronto)*

The interactive Ontario Science Centre, as it was renamed, did not open until the fall of 1969, when a radio signal more than 1.5 billion light years away struck a circuit to raise a curtain. The Centre is situated in a river ravine about eleven kilometres from downtown, the architecture fitting into the natural contours of the site. More than a hundred and fifty thousand school children visit each year. Altogether, the Centre has received more than fifty million visitors.

The Ontario County Courthouse in Whitby was converted into a community centre with a theatre and renamed the Centennial Building as a centennial project in 1967. *Photo: Rick Harris / Flickr*

Manitoba: *Centennial Concert Hall (Winnipeg)*

The 2,305-seat concert hall opened in March 1968. At its opening, the acoustics were considered to be as good as any in North America. The Winnipeg Symphony Orchestra and the Royal Winnipeg Ballet frequently perform in the hall, which also has been the venue for popular music acts.

Saskatchewan: *Saskatchewan Centre for the Arts (Regina); Saskatoon Centennial Auditorium (Saskatoon)*

The arts complex in Regina, now known as the Conexus Arts Centre, opened in 1970, after construction delays resulting from higher than expected costs. (Engineering students at the nearby university erected a sign declaring the unfinished building to be the "world's largest monkey bars.") The centre has a 2,031-seat concert hall, a convention hall and conference rooms. It is home to the Regina Symphony Orchestra. Saskatoon Centennial Auditorium, now TCU Place, opened in 1968 with a 2,003-seat theatre. It also contains a convention centre.

Alberta: *Provincial Museum of Alberta (Edmonton)*

The Royal Alberta Museum, as it is now known, opened in December 1967, with three main galleries dedicated to the fur trade, Alberta's native peoples, and early photographs of Aboriginal people. The museum now has more than ten million pieces in its collection.

British Columbia: *Royal British Columbia Museum (Victoria)*

The museum opened in August 1968, with permanent galleries dedicated to natural history, modern history, and First Peoples. The museum, located across the street from the Legislature, includes on its grounds historic houses; Thunderbird Park, with replicas of totem poles; and the Netherlands Centennial Carillon with its sixty-two bells, a gift to Canada in Centennial Year, in gratitude for the nation's role in liberating Holland during the Second World War.

Yukon: *MacBride Museum (Whitehorse)*

A log cabin was built in 1967 to house the collection of the MacBride Museum, named for Bill MacBride, an employee of the White Pass and Yukon Route railroad, who had a penchant for collecting artefacts and anecdotes.

Northwest Territories: *Hay River Centennial Library (Hay River)*

The library houses the offices of the Public Library Services, which organize the circulation of the collection among the territories' twenty-one public libraries.

NATIONAL BUILDING PROJECTS

Confederation Centre of the Arts (Charlottetown)
This imposing structure, featuring four concrete cubes occupying a city block, opened in 1964 for the centennial of the Charlottetown Conference. The centre also contains the only national monument to the Fathers of Confederation. Included in the complex are several theatres and an art gallery. At its opening, Prime Minister Lester Pearson stated that the Centre is "dedicated to the fostering of those things that enrich the mind and delight the heart, those intangible but precious things that give meaning to a society and help create from it a civilization and a culture."

The **National Arts Centre** in Ottawa opened on June 2, 1969, with a mandate to present opera, theatre, music and dance in both of Canada's official languages. Initially, it had three performance spaces: the Opera (now Southam Hall, named after the Centre's driving force, Hamilton Southam); the Theatre; and the Studio. The Fourth Stage was added in 2000. The Centre is home to the National Arts Centre Orchestra.

Small Reminders

Centennial projects ranged from those as grand as Expo 67 to those as modest as the renovation of a meeting room in a provincial hamlet.

A typical celebration occurred in Redcliff, Alberta (which borders Medicine Hat); some fifty-six years after its incorporation, the town acquired its first library. A Lions Club civic centre was converted into a 2,000-volume library as part of an $11,000 project. The town raised $6,000, with help from the provincial government, while centennial funds covered the rest.

"It is more than the bricks and mortar," Alberta centennial officer Ted Abell told the audience at the ribbon-cutting ceremony. "It is Canadians working together to get what we want out of the Centennial program."

A variety of small centennial projects improved life in hamlets surrounding Medicine Hat:

- In Schuler, a playground and cairn were erected.
- In Hilda, the curling rink was converted to an indoor skating rink.
- In Irvine, improvements were made to the park and baseball grounds.
- In Seven Persons, a changing room was added to the skating rink.
- In Iddesleigh, a museum was constructed.
- In Suffield, a skating rink was built.

On the Wild Side

UFO LANDING PAD

St. Paul is about 200 kilometres northeast of Edmonton, and about 430 kilometres northwest of Saskatoon. It is a long way from the big city, but as close to outer space as is any other place on earth.

micro-REMINDERS

Charles MacLeod had worked for twenty-nine years in the Canadian National Railways shops in Moncton, New Brunswick. He marked the Centennial by forging miniature steel blacksmith's tools resembling those used by his father, who had opened a smithy in 1875.

A few fellows sitting around drinking beer came up with a centennial project even more audacious than Expo 67. The space race was on, man had yet to stroll on the Moon, and the possibility of confronting extraterrestrial life both appalled and fascinated. So, right in the middle of St. Paul, they began building a landing pad for unidentified flying objects. (If their efforts achieved nothing else, they might at least serve to promote the six-elevator farming town on a prairie crossroads.)

The landing pad, made of concrete and reinforced steel, boasted a platform twelve metres in diameter. (The pad was big enough for "Little Green Men" from the red planet, but not for aliens from, say, *Close Encounters of the Third Kind*.) A welcoming sign read:

> *Republic of St. Paul (Stargate Alpha): The area under the World's First UFO Landing Pad was designated international by the Town of St. Paul as a symbol of our faith that mankind will maintain the outer universe free from national wars and strife. That future travel in space will be safe for all intergalactic beings, all visitors from earth or otherwise are welcome to this territory and to the Town of St. Paul.*

To date, no aliens have landed, but tourists surely have, posing for photographs and purchasing souvenirs at a stand that was added years later. They can also view a map of Canada constructed of stones from each of the provinces. A light marks the location of St. Paul, accompanied by the notation "You are here," which undoubtedly would assist disoriented intergalactic creatures.

monumental concern

A commemorative monument in a park in Grand Falls-Windsor in Newfoundland and Labrador recently has attracted attention, after falling into disrepair. The park has become known primarily as Centennial Park—though, in 1967, it was dedicated as Shawnadithit Centennial Park, named for the last known surviving member of the Beothuk people. Brendan Sheppard, chief of the Qalipu Mi'kmaq First Nation, called upon the municipal government to repair the monument and to refer to the park, both in signage and documents, by the full name adopted in Centennial Year.

The residents of St. Paul, Alberta, didn't just build a bandshell as a civic centennial project. They built a landing pad for flying saucers. Though they have yet to entertain intergalactic visitors, the landing pad remains a popular tourist destination. *Photo: Alberta Rural Physician Action Plan / Flickr*

The lieutenant-governor came to the town for the launching pad's sod-turning ceremony, while Defence Minister Paul Hellyer attended the official opening. (Hellyer later earned derision for his insistence upon the existence of alien life, an opinion perhaps influenced by his time in St. Paul.) The pad was one of seventy-five centennial projects launched by the town of about three thousand people (today, about 5,400). It was declared the Centennial Capital of Canada.

St. Paul was so infused with centennial spirit that they had commemorated the hundredth anniversary of the Charlottetown Conference by sending a cowhide to the Prince Edward Island capital with twenty-three hundred signatures in affirmation of Confederation. The town's celebratory fervour inspired the National Film Board to produce a short documentary, *Centennial Fever, or the Hundred-Year Itch.*

The flying-saucer landing pad remains a popular tourist attraction, competing with Alberta landmarks such as the Giant Perogy in Glendon, the Giant Kielbasa in Mundare and the Giant Grey Geese of Hanna. When not serving extraterrestrial visitors, St. Paul's landing pad serves as a bandstand—though it should not be regarded as such. No one has ever driven hundreds of kilometres across a prairie to see an ordinary bandstand.

SAUCY SECESSION: RATHNELLY

In the pouring rain, a small boy in short pants, wearing a military-style jacket with gold braid and epaulets, an umbrella in his right hand and a toy rifle in his left, marched up the street, splashing with every step.

The boy was a member of the Rathnelly Irregulars, a spontaneously formed militia of the Republic of Rathnelly, a five-square block of central Toronto that declared its secession from Canada as the rest of the nation celebrated Centennial.

According to the *Toronto Star*, independence came as a result of a "bloodless, post-breakfast coup," which was duly toasted by the locals.

Time Capsule for 2017

On October 20, 1967, schoolchildren were let out of class early to join the mayor in placing a time capsule at the new High Prairie and District Museum in Alberta. During the dedication ceremony, it was announced that the time capsule was to be opened in fifty years' time—in 2017, though the exact day was not specified.

The town of High Prairie, located along the historic staging route for the Klondike gold rush, opened the museum as a centennial project.

These are some of the items placed in the time capsule:

- A letter from mayor Terry Anderson, to be read in 2017
- an aerial photograph of High River, Alberta, taken in 1947
- a National Housing Act booklet from 1954
- colour photographs of the town, from 1967
- a Peace River District telephone directory for 1966–67
- three copies of the *South Peace News*
- Expo 67 pamphlets

- a High Prairie voters list
- a spring catalogue from Eaton's
- a catalogue from Massey-Ferguson
- a photograph of contemporary farm machinery
- advertisements for new model cars in 1967
- a blueprint of the town of High Prairie
- an edition of *Time* magazine dated August 18, 1967 (featuring American yachting skipper Bus Mosbacher on the cover).

"As tankards of Rathnellian mead—the republic's only liquid assets—were handed round, statesman met statesman in an attempt to hammer out a treaty," the newspaper reported.

The leafy neighbourhood was home to about four hundred residents—er, citizens. The day's major act, post-coup, was the peaceful seizure of a local water-pumping station in a park that was renamed Freedom Square.

"We planned it as a reminder that there was a slender thread of rebellion in Canada's history," said unrepentant republican Alan Thomas.

A piper led the Irregulars on patrol at street barricades set up around the area between Casa Loma and Avenue Road and north of the Davenport Road railroad tracks. At the time, the neighbourhood faced the prospect

Queen Juliana of the Netherlands is greeted by mayor Steven Juba on her arrival in Winnipeg on a Canadian tour in 1967. *Photo: University of Manitoba Archives & Special Collections*

of being ruined by freeways—a fate avoided when the planned Crosstown and Spadina Expressways were cancelled some years later.

Two years later, the leaders of the fledgling "republic" wrote a letter to Prime Minister Pierre Trudeau: "Because we are a developing nation both in size and members, our voice is somewhat small, but with time we shall make up in influence what we lack in power," D.C. Hayes wrote. "As a Canadian, you can appreciate our position."

He complained of a territorial violation on the part of city works crews that insisted upon using the water-pumping plant. The "republic" offered to grant use of this land to the city in exchange for a Canadian foreign-aid grant of $123.29, for the purchase of playground equipment.

Noting that the city recently had erected a statue of Edward VII astride his horse, the Rathnellians also requested funds for a statue of "republic" founder Ambrose J. Small facing backward on a donkey.

The prime minister respectfully declined, suggesting that the "republic" temporarily dissolve, in order to seek municipal aid.

The tongue-in-cheek notion of the nation-for-a-day is revived during biannual neighbourhood block parties, and has been a running joke now for half a century.

The idea of the "republic" was inspired by the British comedy *Passport to Pimlico*, a movie that took its cue from the temporary wartime designation of a maternity ward in Ottawa as Dutch territory so that the birth of Princess Juliana on "Dutch" soil would permit her eligibility for the throne.

Bubbles, a poodle, won election as head of state, but an inability to follow commands—or to issue them, for that matter—led to a resident named Fred Fisher's serving as honorary president. He wore a top hat, opera cape, tuxedo pants and no shoes. All children aged five to fourteen were conscripted into the Irregulars.

The "republic" held a coronation for Eileen Robertson, known as "Eileen I," who had moved onto Rathnelly Avenue in 1924. The street took its name from the estate built for Canadian Senator William McMaster, who named it after his birthplace in Ireland.

One of the first acts of the "republic" was the creation of a coat of arms. The four panels depicted train tracks, six martini glasses, the five city blocks and the Expo 67 logo. As well as issuing passports, the enclave adopted a national anthem ("Rathnelly the Brave") and launched an "air farce" consisting of a thousand helium balloons. One year they even held an Expo of their own, with individual houses decorated to represent national pavilions.

In 2012, the city good-naturedly introduced special street signs heralding the "republic," complete with its coat of arms, as though the Republic of Rathnelly were a legitimate historical neighbourhood like Leslieville or Little Italy.

The denizens decided to mark the fiftieth anniversary of their secession by declaring a Republic of Love on June 17, 2017, encouraging all former residents to return to the homeland for the day.

TOQUE TROUBLE

One centennial project in High River, Alberta—the making and selling of centennial toques to finance hockey trips for the local peewees—earned a spot in *Hansard* when the local member of Parliament showed up in the House of Commons wearing one, a violation of the dress code that occasioned an exchange with the Speaker.

Photo Credits

LIBRARY AND ARCHIVES CANADA

Photos © Government of Canada. Reproduced with the permission of Library and Archives Canada (2017)

iv   Library and Archives Canada/Library and Archives Canada Miscellaneous Poster Collection/e010779398

vii   Library and Archives Canada/Canadian Corporation for the 1967 World Exhibition fonds/e000990869

4   Library and Archives Canada/ Library and Archives Canada Miscellaneous Poster Collection/e010779402

7   Library and Archives Canada/Canadian Corporation for the 1967 World Exhibition fonds/e000990889

25   Library and Archives Canada/Library and Archives Canada Miscellaneous Poster Collection/e010779413

46   Library and Archives Canada/Library and Archives Canada Miscellaneous Poster Collection/e010779429

48   Library and Archives Canada/Centennial Commission fonds/e001098956

63   Library and Archives Canada/Centennial Commission fonds/a185511

85   Library and Archives Canada/Centennial Commission fonds/C-024559

91   Library and Archives Canada/Centennial Commission fonds/a091062

96   Library and Archives Canada/Canadian Corporation for the 1967 World Exhibition fonds/e000990924

99   Library and Archives Canada/Canadian Corporation for the 1967 World Exhibition fonds/e000996546

101   Library and Archives Canada/Canadian Corporation for the 1967 World Exhibition fonds/e000996547

103   Library and Archives Canada/Centennial Commission fonds/e001098960

107   Library and Archives Canada/Canadian Corporation for the 1967 World Exhibition fonds/e000990923

110   Library and Archives Canada/Canadian Corporation for the 1967 World Exhibition fonds/e000990908

113   Library and Archives Canada/Centennial Commission fonds/e001098962

126   Library and Archives Canada/Department of Health fonds/e011161222

127   top Library and Archives Canada/Department of Health fonds/e011161211

127   bottom Library and Archives Canada/Department of Health fonds/e011161208

131   Library and Archives Canada/Centennial Commission fonds/a185522

136   Library and Archives Canada/Department of Health fonds/e011156772

148   Library and Archives Canada/Canadian Corporation for the 1967 World Exhibition fonds/e000995990

149   Library and Archives Canada/Canadian Corporation for the 1967 World Exhibition fonds/e001096652

152   top Library and Archives Canada/Canadian Corporation for the 1967 World Exhibition fonds/e000996022

154   top Library and Archives Canada/Canadian Corporation for the 1967 World Exhibition fonds/e000990910

154   bottom Library and Archives Canada/Canadian Corporation for the 1967 World Exhibition fonds/e000988792

155   Library and Archives Canada/Centennial Commission fonds/C-030085

Acknowledgments

THE IDEA FOR this book percolated for several months. It came into clearer focus after my friend Gordon McIntyre visited his home province on the prairies. Among the images he took was one of an impossibly weathered shack. Above the door was a familiar symbol, a stylized maple leaf consisting of triangles. This was the Centennial Fire Hall of Sovereign, Saskatchewan. It was in that moment I realized the full scope of the centennial celebrations. The party touched every dot on the map.

I owe thanks to the reporters and authors who earlier reported and reflected on the meaning of the Centennial and Expo 67. A special nod to Robert Fulford, as insightful an observer today as he was a half-century ago. It was also a joy to read the *Weekend Magazine* work of both Bob Stall, a former colleague, and the late Patrick Nagle, a mentor who is missed by his many old friends.

This project included several interviews in which the conversation started, "How did you track me down?" There are a lot of Gallants in Prince Edward Island, but only one Hank Gallant of Nail Ponds. Hank's detailed recall of his trans-Canada walk had me in stitches. He deserves more credit for his astonishing feat and here's hoping this book settles accounts in his favour.

Heather Cooper, an artist who designed the famous beaver logo for the Roots clothing store, offered helpful anecdotes of her trip with other youth to Europe to spread the word of Canada. June Charette's memories of her father Stan Guignard's abortive around-the-world trip in a Model T Ford were much appreciated. Ray Chipeniuk's mountain-climbing stories about his late friend Erik Sheer helped put in context Sheer's desire to climb Mount Kilimanjaro as a boy. Sandra Kathnelson, who may have been the first newborn in 1967 to be described in print by her parents as a centennial project, told me about her accomplished family. Tara Ney and Frank D. Ney added information about their father, the late Frank Ney, swashbuckling mayor and instigator of the bathtub race in Nanaimo, BC. Others who offered helpful information about people and projects in this book include Val Cline and Dr. Georges Terroux.

Meaghan Beaton's writings about Nina Cohen were informative and inspirational. Cohen, a philanthropist with selfless drive, was responsible for the founding of both the Men of the Deeps choir and the Miners' Museum in Glace Bay on Cape Breton Island in Nova Scotia.

In his own works about Canada's rock history, Bob Mersereau tracked down from the source himself, Gordon Lightfoot, the story about how the remarkable "Canadian Railway Trilogy" came to be commissioned. Thanks for permission to quote the anecdote here.

Even a light-hearted book such as this has a million small facts to be checked (and double-checked), so I'm grateful to Brian Grant Duff and countless others for sharing their expertise. Melanie Macdonald, Rod McDonald, and P.J. MacDougall, the librarian at Massey College in Toronto, helped provide information on the late typographer Carl Dair. Thanks, too, to Kate Heartfield and Kurt Johnson for assistance in telling Kurt's story about hitchhiking across Canada on behalf of his fellow citizens of Timmins, Ontario.

It is my good fortune to have among my friends many writers and journalists who are pack rats. Thanks to Caitlin Smith for the copy (now ragged) of the Expo 67 Official Guide and to Jean Baird for the centennial book that once belonged to Al Purdy. Another totem for this project was a small melamine candy dish depicting the Quebec pavilion at Expo 67, a gift from Valerie Murray and Dr. Bryan Murray, friends who also offered two dinners with wonderful conversation during this project. The incomparable Kate Andrew sent her family's collection of centennial posters, while her husband, Marcus Gee, offered helpful suggestions, as he has done since our days together on the *Ubyssey* student newspaper. Kim Westad and Adrian Brooks toasted the (semi-) completion of the first draft with champagne, which places them high in any writer's pantheon. I am blessed to have such unwavering friends and supporters.

A book comes together with a million small kindnesses, so thanks, too, to Matt Adamson, Tom Barrett, Ted Blades, Frances Bula, Susan Delacourt, Chris Gainor, Terry Glavin, Colin Holt, Nicholas Jennings, Bob (Pepito) Krieger, Roy MacGregor, John Mackie and Fiona McQuarrie. Gerry Porter, a legend in Newfoundland and Labrador arts and journalism circles, offered suggestions for this book even as he was dying of brain cancer. His physical absence from our lives is an ache that will long remain.

My editor, Cheryl Cohen, reshuffled the deck when presented with the manuscript, making it an infinitely better work. Her good humour in the face of adversity is a model for all editors. Copy editor Lisa Ferdman rooted out bad sentences, poor word choices and occasional errors. The gang at Douglas and McIntyre have been unstintingly encouraging even as we faced the tightest of deadlines. Nicola Goshulak offered a final polish. Shed Simas performed yeoman's work in tracking down photographs and getting rights for the many terrific images. The unflappable Anna Comfort O'Keeffe kept a steady hand on the tiller throughout.

This book was written before, after and at lunch during shifts at Munro's Books in Victoria, BC. The bookstore is a special physical space (a renovated heritage bank building) with a special staff. The ownership team, led by Jessica Walker, is a joy (and those who know me know how rare are my praises for bosses). A special thanks to scheduler Ellen Squires for a juggling act in which hours and days were found for me to complete the manuscript. Store manager Jessica Paul and my thoughtful, well-read and wickedly funny co-workers make going to work each day a delight.

At home, our South Korean homestay student Eunbi Kim endured endless anecdotes about this country and a year long before her birth.

My mother, Joyce Hawthorn, is responsible for giving me an early love of reading, a lifelong gift, while my late father, whose name I carry, taught me there is no such thing as too many books. My sister, Heather Hawthorn-Doyle, and her family have always been supportive.

This book is dedicated to my children, John Hawthorn and Nellie Hawthorn, who are wonderful young adults, as is Nellie's partner, Tyler Clarke. Finally, Debbie Wilson endured a living room overwhelmed by books, magazines and newspaper clippings. She offers wise counsel for a writer's dilemmas and has a journalist's skill for getting to the heart of the story. (She once won a lighthearted contest among our friends for best short obituary with: "Tom's dead. Free books.") Simply put, this project would not have been completed without her.

Errors inevitably creep into any work. That's my fault. I'm keen on being kept informed. Send complaints and corrections to tomhawthorn@gmail.com.

For a list of sources and further information, visit http://www.douglas -mcintyre.com/book/the-year-canadians-lost-their-minds-and-found -their-country.

Index